I0649170

R. Wardlaw Thompson

British Foreign Missions, 1837-1897

R. Wardlaw Thompson

British Foreign Missions, 1837-1897

ISBN/EAN: 9783743309111

Manufactured in Europe, USA, Canada, Australia, Japa

Cover: Foto ©ninafisch / pixelio.de

Manufactured and distributed by brebook publishing software
(www.brebook.com)

R. Wardlaw Thompson

British Foreign Missions, 1837-1897

British
Foreign Missions

1837—1897

By

Rev. R. WARDLAW THOMPSON

Foreign Secretary to the London Missionary Society

AND

Rev. ARTHUR N. JOHNSON, M.A.

Home Secretary to the London Missionary Society

LONDON

BLACKIE & SON, Limited, 50 OLD BAILEY, E.C.

GLASGOW AND DUBLIN

1899

Preface

The aim of this book, as indicated by its title, *British Foreign Missions, 1837–1897*, is to give a brief account of the growth and progress of British Foreign Missions during those sixty years of Her Majesty's reign.

The Introductory chapter gives a short account of British missions up to the year 1837. Chapters II. and III. set forth the advance of these missions in the East, Africa, America, and the Pacific Islands. The next five chapters, IV. V. VI. VII. and VIII., describe the special developments which have been made, viz. Education, Medical Missions, Woman's Work, Literature, and Native Churches. The last chapter, IX., sums up the present position. In the Appendix statistics of the leading societies will be found, which the authors have endeavoured to record as accurately as possible.

The subject of the book excluded the large and important work done by societies belonging to the continent of Europe and the United States of America; but the incidental references made to some of them may indicate the vast services rendered by such societies. If their operations were fully described they would be found at least to equal, if not to surpass, those that are recorded here.

Missions to the Jews also did not appear to come within the purpose set before the authors. Lack of space has prevented the description of the many individual and personal missions which British subjects are carrying on in various parts of the field.

The authors gratefully acknowledge the readiness with which the secretaries of many societies have responded to their requests for information, and hereby thank them for their kindness. They would especially mention the valuable assistance rendered by the Rev. J. Gordon Watt, M.A., of the Bible Society, in the compilation of the chapter on Literature (VII.).

They trust that the book, which is furnished with a full Index, will prove to be a useful summary of the great progress and encouraging results achieved by the leading British agencies for the evangelization of the world.

Contents

Contents

CHAPTER III

Growth during the past Sixty Years—The Two Atlantic Continents, and the Islands of the Pacific- - - - 74

Contents

CHAPTER IV

CHAPTER V

Contents

APPENDIX

Statistics of the Chief British Missionary Societies for the year 1897-98

British Foreign Missions.

Chapter I.

Introductory.

Whenever and wherever a man or a community has grasped the meaning of Christ's work and has lived under the influence of a true faith in Him, the desire to preach the gospel to the unevangelized and the ignorant has become marked. Thus it has happened that every period of revived faith has become a period of quickened enterprise, and even in the darkest days of unbelief or of coldness there have been a few earnest hearts concerned about the salvation of their neighbours and looking out wistfully upon the world. Modern missionary enterprise on the continent of Europe was the child of pietism. It found its most remarkable illustration in the Moravian Church, of which it could be said " The *Unitas Fratrum* and missions are inseparably connected. There is never a church of the Brethren without a mission to the heathen, nor a mission of the Brethren which is not an affair of the church as such." [1]

Missionary enterprise in Great Britain sprang out of the Puritan movement. Attention was first drawn to the ignorant and heathen condition of the tribes of Indians in North America with whom the early colonists came into contact. The seal of the Puritan colony of Massachusetts (A.D. 1628) has the device of an Indian

---

[1] Convention of the General Synod, 1869, § 13, quoted by Warneck.

with a scroll in his mouth bearing the words, "Come over and help us". In 1644 a petition was presented to the Long Parliament praying that something might be done for the spread of the gospel in America and the West Indies. This led to the formation in 1649 of the "Society for the Propagation of the Gospel in New England". Cromwell warmly supported the movement, and a collection was ordered to be made throughout England. This realized £12,000. After the Restoration the society was reconstituted as "The Royal Corporation for the Propagation of the Gospel in New England". Its first missionary was the saintly and now celebrated John Eliot, known as the "Apostle of the Indians". He was a clergyman at Duxbury in Massachusetts, and resigned his position that he might devote himself to the mission to the heathen. "This (says Warneck) is the first mission to the heathen in the Evangelical Church conducted in an evangelical spirit and blessed with lasting results." The New England Company contributed £50 a year for the support of Eliot and of others who joined and followed him. Another missionary supported by this society was the Rev. John Sergeant, who began his work among the Indians in 1734, and who in 1743 evolved a scheme of an industrial mission, which foreshadowed some of the latest developments of missionary enterprise during the present century, and which, if it had been adequately and earnestly supported, might have had great results. Jonathan Edwards succeeded Sergeant as an agent of the New England Company, and during his missionary life composed his famous treatise on the "Freedom of the Will".

In 1740 an association in Scotland for the promotion of Christian knowledge began to turn its attention to mission work among the Indians. Its first missionary was David Brainerd. He began his work in 1743, and died in 1747, having crowded into that brief period a wonderful record of heroic devotion and self-sacrifice, and having been instrumental in a most remarkable spiritual awakening. The missions of this association continued until the end of last century, though always on a very limited scale. In the meantime two other societies had been formed, which have survived to the present day, and both of which have been enabled to do a very large and important mission work. The "Society for the Promotion of Christian Knowledge" was founded in 1699, and though, as its name denotes, its object has been rather to diffuse information through the publication and circulation of Christian literature than to engage in direct mission work, it was instrumental for many years in largely maintaining that Danish mission which was the first effort to carry the gospel to India, and which had so remarkable a history in South India until its work was taken over by others during the present century. The "Society for the Propagation of the Gospel" was founded in 1701. "The charter shows that the society was incorporated for the three-fold object of (1) providing a maintenance for an orthodox clergy in the plantations, colonies, and factories of Great Britain beyond the seas, for the instruction of the king's loving subjects in the Christian religion; (2) making such other provision as may be necessary for the propagation of the gospel in those parts; and (3) receiving, managing, and disposing of the charity of His Majesty's subjects for these purposes." [1]

The clergy sent out by the Society for the Propagation of the Gospel, or aided by them, devoted themselves mainly to the spiritual needs of the colonists, from whom they derived their chief support; but they were in many cases evidently zealous in caring for the negro and Indian slaves, and also in working among the free

[1] Digest of S.P.G. Records, p. 7.

Indians. They can, however, scarcely be regarded as missionaries to the heathen in the modern acceptation of the term.

On the death of General Codrington in 1710 the society became the trustee of his estates in Barbados, and in the administration of them made earnest and successful efforts for the enlightenment and christianizing of the negro slaves on the estates. Beyond this, they had practically no connection with the West Indies during the whole of the century. They also had a slight connection with West Africa, which is interesting from the fact that one of three negro boys who were sent to England for education in 1757, named Philip Quaque, "became the first of any non-European race since the Reformation to receive Anglican ordination, and on May 17, 1765, he attended the society with his letters of orders, and was appointed missionary, schoolmaster, and catechist to the negroes on the Gold Coast ".[1]

" Though his labours did not show much fruit, Mr. Quaque continued in the mission until his death in 1816, at the age of seventy-five. In token of their appreciation of his long and faithful services the African Company erected a memorial to him at Cape Coast Castle, testifying that he was employed there for upwards of fifty years as missionary from the society and as chaplain to the factory."[2]

Mission work among the negroes of the West Indies was begun by the Moravians at St. Thomas in 1733, but no organized effort for their benefit was made from England until the end of 1786. In that year Dr. Coke and three Wesleyan preachers who were on their way to Nova Scotia were driven by stress of weather to Antigua. They found one or two earnest laymen there who were engaged in voluntary work which, though limited, had already proved very successful.

---

[1] Digest of S.P.G. Records, p. 256.   [2] *Ibid.*, p. 258.

One of the missionaries was at once stationed in Antigua, and missions were also commenced in St. Vincent's, St. Eustatius, Barbados, Tortola, and the Virgin Islands, Jamaica, Bermuda, Bahamas, and St. Domingo. All these missions were inspired and directed by Dr. Coke, who must have been a man of amazing energy and force of character. In these days of rapid and comfortable communication by means of well-appointed steamers, it is not easy to realize what was involved in crossing the Atlantic eighteen times a century ago. He was, during the last thirty years of his life, wholly devoted to the cause of missions. "It was chiefly through his instrumentality that the missions of the Methodists were at first begun, and it was principally by his activity that they were for many years supported and carried on."

Dr. Coke died on a voyage to Ceylon, whither he was conducting a party of missionaries in 1813, to commence a Wesleyan mission on that island.

Practically the whole of British effort on behalf of missions to the heathen during the eighteenth century is summed up in the meagre record just given. No more significant evidence of the feeble and limited nature of this effort can be found than the fact that the income of the Society for the Propagation of the Gospel, which was £1537 in the year of its formation (1701), had actually dwindled down to £602 in 1800. It had in the latter year dividends amounting to £3378, and special funds, mainly the income of the Codrington estates, which yielded £2477. But the zeal and generosity of its living supporters provided only £602 for its work.

The state of religion in Great Britain was unfavourable to the growth of any missionary enthusiasm or to the maintenance of any missionary effort. Sir William Blackstone (1723–1780), who made a point of hearing all the celebrated preachers in London, states "that in all his visits to the churches he did not hear a sermon that had more Christianity in it than a speech of Cicero's, and that it was impossible for him to tell whether the preacher was a Mohammedan or a Christian".[1]

"Dr. Johnson told Boswell that he had never met a 'religious clergyman'; and as we look round the country in the closing years of the century we see hunting clergy, drinking clergy, pluralist and non-resident clergy; empty churches, and the people spending Sunday in brutal sports; parishes without a Bible in them, and without a school worthy of the name."[2]

The dissenting churches were not in quite so serious a condition as this, but they had to a very large extent lost the fervour and the zeal of earlier days, and had settled down into a condition of spiritual lukewarmness which was destructive of all effort. "Such was the dread of innovation which prevailed among Dissenters at that time that it is difficult to say which were the more hearty opponents of Whitefield and the Wesleys—the bishops or the Nonconformists. To tolerate Arians, or even Socinians, in their churches, was a light crime in those days with Dissenters, compared with countenancing men who preached two or three times every day and sought no other prescriptive rule for their proceedings but the spirit and conduct of the first Christians."[3]

There could be no general interest in missions to the heathen at a time when the general attitude towards religion was a cold intellectual orthodoxy, or a coarse and blatant infidelity; when the people were sunk in the grossest ignorance; when society was shamelessly licentious, and political life was notoriously corrupt.

In the midst of this darkness, however, influences

---

[1] Skeat's *History of the Free Churches*, p. 438.
[2] Eugene Stock, *One Hundred Years*, p. 5.
[3] Morison's *Fathers and Founders of the L.M.S.*, vol. i. 41, 42.

were at work which were destined to revolutionize the whole course of British life, and to which the remarkable development of the missionary enterprise during the present century is directly due. In the first place, a remarkable series of discoveries and inventions following each in quick succession gave a new vitality and a new expansiveness to all the industries of the country. The invention of the spinning-jenny by the weaver Hargreave in 1764, of the spinning-frame by Arkwright in 1768, and of the spinning-mule by Crompton in 1776, was the foundation of modern textile manufactures. The application of the artificial blast in iron furnaces was the beginning of the modern iron trade. The discovery by Watt in 1765 of the principle of the condensing cylinder converted the steam-engine at once from an uncertain toy into one of the most powerful, most reliable, and most generally useful servants of human activity. A great social and economic change was the result of these discoveries, the end of which has not yet been seen.

The immediate result of the steady and increasingly rapid growth of wealth among the manufacturing communities was the rise into a new position of influence of a class of intelligent and enterprising men. The need for new markets followed the cheapening and rapid increase of productions, and out of this grew the amazing development of commercial enterprise during the present century. Then followed the application of steam to locomotion, providing swift and certain means of access to the remotest parts of the world. Thus were provided enormous material resources available for any object which might arouse the interest and stimulate the enthusiasm of the people.

Meanwhile a silent but potent leaven of religious awakening and change was at work, which, when the time came, was to make use of the great mechanical discoveries and of the industrial developments for the propagation of Christianity in the remotest parts of the earth.

In 1736, as Mr. Stock points out in his *Short History of the Church Missionary Society,* Bishop Butler refused the primacy because he thought it too late to save a falling Church. Yet in that year Wesley took that eventful voyage to Georgia as a chaplain from which he was to return a changed man, having been taught by a Moravian missionary the way of salvation by grace. In that year also George Whitefield was ordained. From this time, therefore, may be dated the beginning of that evangelical revival which has been the fountain and the inspiration of modern British missions to the heathen. Opposition was bitter and general, and was as painfully manifest among the religious as among the profane, but the great movement spread continuously. Thousands in many places were brought under deep conviction of sin and found a new life in the proclamation of the doctrines of grace. A small but earnest and influential band of clergy were zealous advocates of evangelical truth, and became distinguished for the devotion and consecration of their lives. Among the Nonconformists also a new zeal for evangelical religion awoke and spread. It is evident that there was in many quarters during the last quarter of the century a growing unrest and a new sense of responsibility and of Christian enterprise which was wanting to find expression.

At this juncture the publication of Captain Cook's journals of his voyages of discovery in the Pacific appeared, telling of islands he had visited, and of the ignorance, heathenism, and moral degradation of fine races who inhabited them. This publication was as the spark to tinder. The Rev. Dr. Haweis, Rector of Aldwinkle, read the book, and immediately resolved to send a mission to the South Sea Islands. In consultation with the Countess of Huntingdon, four men were chosen to be the missionaries, and passage was sought for them in one of His Majesty's ships. If the men had not proved faithless at the last moment this would have been the first distinctly and entirely missionary movement in Britain. William Carey, an obscure Baptist minister in Northamptonshire, read the book, and was stimulated to write, in 1789, his *Enquiry into the Obligations of Christians to use means for the Conversion of the Heathens. In which the Religious State of Different Nations of the World, and the success of former undertakings are considered.*

Already in 1784 a monthly missionary prayer-meeting had been commenced among the Baptist churches in Northamptonshire, and in 1786 the Eclectic Society of Evangelical Churchmen had discussed foreign missions for the first time.

The time had come when the awakened feeling of the evangelical revival must find expression in larger enterprises than those of home evangelization. Perhaps it might with truth be said that being repressed and prevented from finding adequate expression by the conditions of society in Britain, the time had come when the evangelical spirit must find an outlet in the newly-opened world abroad.

The Baptist Missionary Society, founded in 1792, was the result of William Carey's enthusiasm and Andrew Fuller's pleading. It was the earliest of the long succession of societies and organizations by means of which the missionary spirit in the modern church has sought to express itself. The first letters from Carey after he went to India proved the means of crystallizing into form thoughts which had been stirring the heart of the Rev. Dr. Bogue, a Congregational minister at Gosport. The result was the formation in 1795 of the " Missionary

Society ", soon to be known as the London Missionary Society. Dr. Haweis has been justly recognized as one of the prime movers in the formation of the London Missionary Society. Certainly it was his offer of £500 which encouraged Bogue to write his celebrated letter in the *Evangelical Magazine* in 1794, and it was his influence which led to the choice of its first field of labour. The enthusiasm awakened by the formation of the London Missionary Society spread throughout the kingdom, and prompted the formation in the following year, 1796, on the same broad evangelical basis, of the Edinburgh Missionary Society, afterwards known as the Scottish Missionary Society, and also of the Glasgow Missionary Society. In 1799 the Church Missionary Society, originally styled the Society for Missions to Africa and the East, was formed by a number of evangelical church-men, many of whom were already contributors to the London Missionary Society, but who felt that, as church-men, their responsibilities would be more adequately discharged by carrying on mission work on more strictly ecclesiastical lines. The Methodists did not form a missionary society until 1817, but as early as 1804, when Dr. Coke started for America, Conference entrusted the missionary operations which he had directed to the care of a committee of three. Thus within fifteen years every section of the Evangelical Protestant Church of Great Britain had waked up to a new sense of duty to the heathen, and had definitely embarked upon the great enterprise, the growth of which has been so prominent and remarkable a feature in the religious life of the nine-teenth century. In 1799 the Religious Tract Society came into being, and was followed by the British and Foreign Bible Society in 1804. The new missionary agencies were thus furnished from the outset with two powerful auxiliaries, the value of whose help ever since, and in every part of the world, has been incalculable.

The new movement did not seem to have chosen an auspicious time for its commencement. England had just been compelled to end an unrighteous war against her own colonies by admitting their independence. The horrors of the French Revolution had also just been enacted, and had made sober and timid men fearful of all new movements. One learned lawyer actually said in the course of the debate on foreign missions in the General Assembly of the Church of Scotland, and referring to the newly-formed missionary societies: "Observe, sir, they are affiliated; they have a common object, they correspond with each other, they look for assistance from foreign countries, in the very language of many of the seditious societies. Above all, it is to be marked they have a common fund. As to these missionary societies, I do aver that it is to be apprehended that their funds may be—nay, certainly will be—turned against the Constitution."

The majority of the leaders of religious opinion throughout the kingdom were also either apathetic or hostile. Charles Grant propounded in 1786 his scheme for the establishment by the East India Company of a mission in Bengal, which was to be divided into eight districts, each under the care of a clergyman, who was to be employed in setting up schools, superintending catechists, and forming churches. Grant's scheme was submitted to the Archbishop of Canterbury and the Bishop of London, and both effectually poured cold water on it.

After the formation of the Baptist Missionary Society, Andrew Fuller said, "When we began in 1792 there was little or no respectability among us, not so much as a squire to sit in the chair or an orator to make speeches to him. Hence good Dr. Stennett advised the London ministers to stand aloof and not commit themselves."

Those who had undertaken the great enterprise were, however, inspired with a divine enthusiasm which was well content to accept criticism and opposition as part of the inevitable cost of fidelity to duty. They pressed forward with an energy and determination which, when the conditions of the times are understood, afford a remarkable evidence of faith and courage. The BAPTIST MISSIONARY SOCIETY sent William Carey and Dr. Thomas to India in 1793, and thus commenced what was soon to be known as the Serampore Mission. The work done by this mission, under the direction of Messrs. Carey, Marshman, and Ward, during the first twenty years of its history, still stands out unique in all modern missionary effort. "In the first third of the nineteenth century, during which this mission was the model and stimulus of almost all others, we have these direct spiritual and indirect civilizing results:—The first complete or partial translation of the Bible printed in forty languages and dialects of India, China, Central Asia, and neighbouring lands, at a cost of £80,143; the first prose work and vernacular newspaper in Bengalee, the language of seventy millions of human beings; the first printing-press on an organized scale, paper-mill, and steam-engine seen in India; the first Christian primary school in North India, the first efforts to educate native girls and women; the first college to train native ministers and christianize educated Hindus; the first Hindoo convert, Krishna Chundra Pal, baptized in 1800; the first medical mission, of which that convert was to some extent the fruit; the establishment and maintenance of at least thirty separate large mission stations, besides Judson's great work in Burmah, which resulted in the foundation of the American Baptist Missionary Society; the first private garden, and society for the improvement of native and European agriculture and horticulture in India; the first savings-bank in

India; the first translation into English of the great Sanscrit epics, the *Ramayan* and the *Maha Bharat*, and the first translation of the Bible into Sanskrit." [1]

The Serampore Mission after a time became separated from the Baptist Missionary Society, but continued to work side by side in harmony with it until it was reunited with it in 1858. The society made Calcutta its head-quarters, and gradually extended its work in North India, establishing itself successively in Cutwa and Dinajpur (1804), Jessore (1808), Agra (1811), Bacca and Chittagong (1812), Benares and Monghir (1816), Delhi (1817), Sura Birbhoom (1818), Muttra (1826), and Barisal (1828). Ceylon was also occupied in 1812. A second great mission was commenced by the Baptist Missionary Society in 1816 in the West Indies, and was rapidly extended notwithstanding the violent hostility of a large section of the European population in Jamaica. In 1816 also that section of the Baptist churches in Great Britain known as the General Baptists formed a missionary society of their own. It was five years before this society was able to commence work in consequence of lack of suitable agents. In 1821 their first missionary went out to India, and by the advice of the Serampore missionaries they chose Orissa as their field of labour.

The LONDON MISSIONARY SOCIETY, under the inspiration of Dr. Haweis, turned its attention first to the South Seas. In 1796 it bought a vessel, *The Duff*, and sent her off with a party of thirty missionaries, who commenced a mission on Otaheite, or Tahiti, and another in the Friendly Islands. The latter was broken up by the murder of three of the missionaries and the flight of the five survivors, after " two and a half years of indescribable horror ". The night of toil on Tahiti lasted twelve years, during which the faith of some

[1] Dr. G. Smith, *Short History of Christian Missions*, p. 167.

entirely failed, and they retired to New South Wales in fear and hopelessness. Then, at the darkest hour, came a sudden change, and a fire was kindled which was destined to spread from one end of the Pacific to the other, until, after three-quarters of a century, it finally reached New Guinea. The mission in the Leeward Islands was commenced in 1812. The Austral group was occupied in 1816. The Tuamotu Archipelago became the sphere of native evangelists from Tahiti about the same time. In 1821 the first Christian worker (also a native) landed on Aitutaki, which was the first of the Hervey (or Cook) Group to receive the gospel. John Williams settled the first native teachers in the Navigators (or Samoan) Group in 1830.

In the same year as saw the commencement of the mission to the South Seas, the London Missionary Society attempted, in conjunction with the Edinburgh Missionary Society and the Glasgow Missionary Society, a mission to the Foulahs, on the West Coast of Africa. This effort, however, proved unsuccessful. In 1799 the society sent its first missionary to India. As Carey and his companions were compelled to find a place of residence and sphere of work under the shelter of the Danish flag in consequence of the hostility of the East India Company to missions and missionaries, so Mr. Forsyth found it necessary to make the Dutch settlement of Chinsurah, about twenty miles from Calcutta, his place of abode, though he afterwards extended his labours to Calcutta. He was followed in 1804 by a party of six who landed at Madras. Two of these opened a station at Vizagapatam, three went to Ceylon, and the sixth, the Rev. W. T. Ringeltaube, after a brief residence at Palamcottah, began that mission in Travancore which has been so remarkable an illustration of the renewing and elevating power of the gospel, and with which his name has become inseparably connected. Madras was occupied in the same year. In 1810 the mission at Bellary was commenced. Ten years later (1820) Benares, in the north, and Belgaum and Bangalore, in the west and south, became centres of new work. The mission was further extended in 1822 to Cuddapah, in 1827 to Salem, and in 1830 to Coimbatore. Surat had been one of the first places in India thought of by the society as the centre of a mission, but it was not occupied until 1815.

In 1799 Dr. Van der Kemp landed in South Africa, the first missionary sent by any British society, and the first of a long succession of missionaries who have since laboured in that country in connection with the London Missionary Society. A local association, the South African Missionary Society, was formed at the Cape in 1802 to co-operate with Van der Kemp and his fellow-labourers, and the mission spread in the colony and among the Namaquas. In 1816 the first permanent work among the Kaffirs was begun, and in 1821 Robert Moffat began those labours at Kuruman which made him the apostle of Bechuanaland.

The urgent appeal of a devout Dutch planter in Demerara led to the commencement of the mission in the West Indies in 1807. Berbice followed Demerara in 1813, and the mission was extended to Jamaica in 1834. In 1818 the two first missionaries were sent to Madagascar, and, between that time and the death of Radama I. in 1828, fourteen others were sent to join them. A printing-press was set up at the capital, at which the entire Bible, translated by the missionaries, was printed. Mission schools were established, and instruction in the industrial arts was given by lay agents sent out for that purpose. In 1835 the missionaries were compelled to leave the island. In July, 1837, the profession of Christianity was forbidden.

Christian worship prohibited, and every book confiscated.

The CHURCH MISSIONARY SOCIETY had a feeble beginning, which gave no promise of that great subsequent development which has at length won for it undisputed and universal recognition as the greatest of British Protestant missionary organizations. Its first leaders and supporters, John Venn, Thomas Scott, William Wilberforce, Charles Grant, and others, were men of large hearts, broad and sound conceptions of duty, and fearless courage, but they had to wait sixteen months after the formation of the society before they received the imprimatur and sanction of the Archbishop of Canterbury, and it was *four years* before they could get any suitable candidates to offer themselves for missionary service. The first field entered by the Church Missionary Society was West Africa; two missionaries being sent to the Susoo tribes on the Rio Pongas in 1802. In 1816 this mission was given up in favour of Sierra Leone, where work was begun, at the request of the British Government, among the liberated slaves. In 1809, on the appeal of one whose true greatness as a Christian pioneer has never yet been fully recognized, the Rev. Samuel Marsden, M.A., the colonial chaplain at Paramatta, New South Wales, it was resolved to begin a mission among the Maoris of New Zealand, but the first missionaries did not actually enter upon their work until Christmas 1814. Two men, brothers, named Henry and William Williams, who went out in 1822 and 1828, proved to be the evangelists of the Maori race and the founders of the colony. "They landed in New Zealand before there was a single convert, and when no colonists dare settle there for fear of the cannibals. They lived to see the whole Maori people brought under the sound of the gospel, thousands of true converts brought into the Church, and hundreds dying in the faith of Christ; and they lived to see a great British colony in one of the finest climates in the world." [1]

An earnest band of Christian chaplains and laymen in North India were in close sympathy with the work of the Church Missionary Society, and a corresponding committee was early formed in Calcutta. The society's connection with India was commenced through the instrumentality of this committee in 1813 by the appointment of a native, Abdul Masih, a convert won by Henry Martyn, to work at Agra. The four first missionaries were appointed in 1814, two of whom went to Calcutta, while the other two commenced work in Benares and Meerut. In South India the society began in 1820 by taking charge from the Society for the Promotion of Christian Knowledge of the old Danish Mission in the Tamil country. One of the two missionaries appointed to this mission was Rhenius. Under his influence the work wonderfully revived, and in 1829 was handed over to the care of the Society for the Propagation of the Gospel. Meanwhile Rhenius had been preaching and gathering converts and congregations in many heathen villages, and these became the nucleus of the great Tinnevelly Mission of the Church Missionary Society. In 1816 a mission was begun in North Travancore and Cochin at the solicitation of Colonel Munro, the British Resident. In 1820 Bombay was occupied, and the mission in the Deccan was commenced in 1822.

The mission to Ceylon was inaugurated in 1817. In 1822 an adventurous missionary found his way to a trading post on the Red River, south of Lake Winnipeg, and thus began that mission in North-west America which was destined in after years to attain to such large dimensions.

Though the WESLEYAN MISSIONARY SOCIETY was not

[1] E. Stock, *One Hundred Years*, p. 44.

founded until 1817, mission work under the auspices of the Wesleyan Conference had been steadily extending before that time. Mention has already been made of the death of Dr. Coke in 1813, during a voyage to Ceylon with a party of missionaries whom he was leading to found a mission in that island. A mission was begun in West Africa at Sierra Leone in 1811, and on the River Gambia in 1821. The first Wesleyan missionary to South Africa landed in 1814. Barnabas Shaw pushed up to Namaqualand in 1816, and began those remarkable labours which he continued for fifty years. In 1820 work was begun in Cape Town, and also in Graham's Town, and was shortly after extended to Kaffirland by William Shaw. In 1821 a party of missionaries went out to commence work in New Zealand, and in the following year the mission to Tonga in the Friendly Islands was begun. From Tonga the work spread in 1835 to Fiji.

The Society for the Propagation of the Gospel did not awake for some time from the torpor into which it had settled in the latter half of the eighteenth century, and attempted very little direct mission work. Its first sustained effort in India was in 1818, when it voted £5000 to Bishop Middleton of Calcutta for missionary purposes. In the following year it gave £45,000 towards the establishment of Bishop's College. In 1826 it took over in Madras the work which had been previously supported by the Society for the Promotion of Christian Knowledge. In 1829 its connection with Tinnevelly began, and Bombay was occupied in 1830. A chaplain was sent out to Cape Town in 1820, and thus work in South Africa was commenced.

The two Scottish societies, founded in Edinburgh and Glasgow in 1796, did not grow so rapidly, and never attained the strength of their contemporaries in England, and ultimately, after about fifty years, they were both absorbed into one or other of the missions which had in the meantime been commenced by different branches of the Presbyterian Church. During their existence, however, they both did valuable work. The Edinburgh or Scottish Missionary Society sent its first missionaries to West Africa in 1798, and on the failure of that mission it opened another in 1802 in the country between the Black and Caspian Seas. This was continued until 1824. In 1822 its Indian Mission was commenced by the Rev. Donald Mitchell, and ultimately made its head-quarters at Bombay and Poonah. Though the mission was a small one, it numbered among its workers the Rev. John Wilson, D.D., of Bombay, one of the greatest of modern missionaries. This Indian Mission was transferred to the Church of Scotland in 1835. In 1824 the Scottish Missionary Society began work in Jamaica, and continued its mission in that island until 1847, when it was transferred to the United Presbyterian Church, and the society came to an end.

The Glasgow Missionary Society turned its attention at once to West Africa, but both members of the first party speedily turned to secular pursuits, and both members of the second party died within six months, so that the mission came to an end. For twenty years the society was dormant, but then revived again, and an important mission was begun in 1824 in Kaffraria. This grew amid many discouragements, but was ultimately divided into two parts and absorbed into the missions of the Free Church of Scotland and the United Presbyterian Church.

A striking evidence of the change of feeling in regard to missions to the heathen is furnished by the action of the Church of Scotland. At a meeting of the General Assembly in 1796 overtures to consider the advisability of undertaking a mission to the heathen and to sanction collections for missions were dismissed, after a long and heated debate, by a majority of fourteen. In 1824 the question of the propagation of Christianity in heathen countries was raised again, and a committee was appointed to consider the subject. They reported in the following year that it was advisable that a mission should be commenced, that one of the provinces of India should be the sphere of its operations, and that its methods should be mainly educational. Out of this report came the commencement of the Church of Scotland's mission to India. The first missionary sent out was the Rev. Alexander Duff, who went to Calcutta in 1829, and of whom it is perhaps no exaggeration to say that to him more than to any other man India owes the great educational provision which has since been given to it.

The conditions were certainly not favourable during the early years of the century to the rapid extension of missions to the heathen. At home the war with France, which continued with one brief respite until the downfall of Napoleon in 1815, denuded the country of men and treasure, and brought a burden of debt and taxation so enormous that universal distress prevailed. The National Debt in 1816 amounted to upwards of £900,000,000, or £45 per head of the population. At present it is less than £16 per head. The political unrest and agitation of the years following the war, to the adoption of the first Reform Bill in 1832, was scarcely less paralysing to religious enthusiasm than the financial burdens of earlier years

Abroad the state of the world was not more promising. The greater part was still entirely closed to all communication, or was so difficult of access from various causes that mission work was prevented. The effort to introduce the gospel to China, made by the London Missionary Society in 1807, apparently failed. Dr. Morrison certainly did a work of unique importance for the future by his preparation of a Chinese dictionary, and by his translation of the Scriptures, but he was only able to accomplish this work under the protection of the East India Company, and within the walls of their trading factory at Canton. When he died in 1834 at Canton, foreigners were excluded from the whole of China more rigidly than ever. The companions and colleagues who had been sent out to join him were compelled to live and work in the Straits Settlements, waiting for the coming of the day which their faith led them to expect, when the barriers which prevented them from entering China should be removed. Japan was even more closely shut and barred against foreigners than China, and remained in this seclusion for many years.

The East India Company strove hard to make Christian missions impossible within the company's domains in India. Notwithstanding the earnest efforts of a small group of godly men who strove to influence and change their policy, they acted consistently in the spirit of the statement made by the Court of Governors in May, 1793, "that the conversion of 50,000 or 100,000 natives of any degree of character would be the most serious disaster that could happen, and they thanked God it was impracticable". They subsidized Hinduism lavishly, in all parts of the country. They took the great temple of Kalighat so completely under their care that it became practically a government institution. They provided guards of honour and fired salutes when idols were carried in procession. But they did their best to keep Christian missionaries out of the country. This attitude was only changed slowly and by compulsion, and was only finally abandoned by the force of public opinion after the Charter was renewed in 1833.

Slavery prevailed in the West Indies and in South Africa, and it was very soon discovered by the slave-owners that while Christianity might make the individual slave more industrious, better behaved, and obedient, it brought with it a new leaven of knowledge and of awakened self-respect which made the permanent continuance of slavery impossible.   A large majority of the planters in the West Indies and in South Africa became bitterly opposed to missions, and sought, partly by legislative enactments and partly by open violence, to prevent the missionaries from teaching their people. The agitation on behalf of the slaves, carried on by Wilberforce and other philanthropists, and which resulted, after many years' struggle, in the great Emancipation Act of 1834, was a splendid object-lesson in practical Christianity to the people of Great Britain, and the payment of £20,000,000 by the British taxpayer as a compensation to the slave-owners was a noble exhibition of principle.   But the agitation, while it lasted, did not tend to make Christian work easier in those places where slavery existed.

Africa, beyond the contracted limits of the Cape Colony and a few isolated places on the coast, was all unknown save as the happy hunting-ground for the detestable traffic in human flesh.

It is not easy to obtain any accurate statistics of the position of foreign missions on the eve of Her Majesty's accession, because the Society for the Propagation of the Gospel and the Wesleyan Missionary Society regarded all their work outside Great Britain as mission work, and consequently included a considerable number of chaplains and ministers to European congregations among their missionaries, and many schools and scholars of European children, and many European communicants, in their general totals.   The whole amount raised for missions to the heathen from all sources did not exceed £300,000.   Five hundred missionaries represented the zeal of all sections of the Protestant Church in Great Britain. The number of communicants connected with mission churches did not exceed 30,000, and not more than 100,000 children were under tuition.

Chapter II.

Growth during the past Sixty Years, especially in India and the East.

So remarkable has been the development of missionary activity during the reign of Her Majesty Queen Victoria that it will be impossible to give any detailed account of the operations of the various societies and organizations which have been formed in connection with foreign missions. The older societies have, with three exceptions, preserved their identity, continued their labours, and greatly extended their operations. The Edinburgh and Glasgow societies were after a time absorbed into newly-formed missions connected with the three Presbyterian churches of Scotland. The General Baptist Missionary Society continued a separate body until 1891, when it was united with the Baptist Missionary Society. Some features of this development of missionary energy are deserving of special notice. There has been in every section of the Church a growing recognition of the principle that the duty of carrying the gospel to the heathen is one of the essential and necessary conditions of Christian life, and not merely a privilege which may or may not be enjoyed at will. One of the most striking and significant evidences of this is in the corporate action of the various branches of the Presbyterian Church. They have in every case accepted the principle that the foreign mission is a distinct branch of the Church's activity as truly as home missions or the support of the ministry, and instead of forming missionary societies of those who are interested in missions they have definitely adopted foreign missions as a distinct and prominent part of the organization of the whole Church and as the duty of every member. Side by side with the development of this principle has been the remarkable springing up of missions which represent individual enthusiasm apart from any particular church relation, or which are specially devoted to some particular branch of mission service.

This enlargement of missionary zeal and activity may be traced, as was the commencement of modern missionary activity in the previous century, to the combined operation of several causes. Powerful influences have been at work to quicken and to elevate the Christian life of Great Britain. The "Oxford Movement", under Keble, Newman, and Pusey, was in progress at the time of the Queen's accession, and whatever other results may have followed it, no one can doubt that the High Church revival has been the means of greatly increasing the learning, the piety, and the devotedness of the clergy of the Church of England, and thus through them of stimulating the laity of the Church to greater consecration. The disruption in the Church of Scotland which created the Free Church in 1843 shook the whole Presbyterian Church out of lethargy and moderatism, and kindled a fire of religious zeal and earnestness which has not since been quenched.

The various movements within the Wesleyan body which have resulted in the hiving-off of successive sections have all helped to stimulate activity of religious thought and earnestness of conviction. Efforts to promote revivals of religion and movements for the deepening of the spiritual life have operated powerfully in the same direction. Every section of the evangelical

Protestant Church has been aroused to a greater spiritual activity, and has recognized afresh and more clearly its duty to spread the Kingdom of Christ.

These spiritual movements, however, would not have availed to effect the work which has been done in the mission field had there not been contemporaneously with them a series of political and economic changes which have completely transformed the face of the world. The development of steam navigation; the Emancipation Act; the revision of the East India Company's Charter in 1833; the Indian Mutiny in 1857; the opening of China, and afterwards of Japan and Korea, to free communication with the world; the progress of exploration by which Africa has been revealed to the world; the extension of Imperial rule in British North America and elsewhere; and above all, the ceaseless enterprise of the missionary spirits of the Church, which has continually anticipated trade and outrun the flag and found admittance through open door after door which had been previously closed, have made the past sixty years a period of remarkable development and of ever-growing fruitfulness in British missions to the heathen.

In 1837 the solitary missionaries of the Church Missionary Society on the Red River in the Hudson's Bay territory depended for communication with England upon the annual voyage of the company's vessel. In the following year the first two steamers crossed from Great Britain to America. They were the pioneers of a rapid and wonderful revolution in the means and frequency of communication. Several steamship companies were at once started, including the Cunard and the Peninsular and Oriental; and it was not many years before steam supplanted the sailing ships on every great trade route as a means of conveying passengers. The change has had a most marked effect upon the facility and economy of the transport of missionaries, and has thus made the provision for the ever-extending field of missionary labour very much easier and communication and supervision more regular and more effective than was possible in the days of sailing vessels.

The abolition of slavery by the Emancipation Act of 1834 was another of the events which made the beginning of the Queen's reign remarkable in relation to missions. The Act did not come into full operation until 1838, and its results were certainly in many cases unsatisfactory at first. The condition of the emancipated people was degraded in the extreme. They were deplorably ignorant, heathen superstitions of the grossest kind dominated their minds; they were habituated to deceit and dishonesty, and were given over to immorality, with hardly any family life amongst them. From the date of the Emancipation Act missionary operations received a great impetus. The Society for the Propagation of the Gospel commenced missions in the West Indies and British Guiana. In the West Indies, to meet the desire of the negroes for instruction, "a special fund was raised called the Negroes' Education Fund. In the next seventeen years the Society for the Propagation of the Gospel expended £172,000 on this object. In 1840 the Colonial Legislature doubled the number of island curacies in Jamaica, and increased the clerical stipends." [1]

The Church Missionary Society commenced a mission in Jamaica in 1834, and it made such rapid progress that when in 1842 the society, in consequence of great financial difficulties, determined to withdraw from the field, "it left an active 'going concern', with excellent men to work it, to the Colonial Church". The London Missionary Society, which had long had a mission in British Guiana, also entered Jamaica in 1834,

[1] Tucker, *English Church in other Lands*, p. 56.

and for many years maintained a strong mission in the island. The Baptist Missionary Society and the Presbyterian missions were also greatly reinforced.

All this was done despite the hostility of the planters. They had given expression to their feeling very unmistakably before emancipation. They became more violent afterwards, and their treatment of the missionaries was often scandalous. A negro rebellion in Morant Bay, Jamaica, resulted in the appointment of a Royal Commission of Inquiry, which absolved the missionaries of blame, and condemned the planters for their conduct. Legislative changes were then begun in which the interests of all classes were guarded, and religion as well as social improvement was promoted.

The freed negroes have, as a result of these changes, steadily improved in intelligence and in Christian character and zeal. The churches in Jamaica connected with the Baptist Missionary Society became independent of that society in 1846. In 1868 the Episcopal Church in the West Indies was disestablished and disendowed. "The heavy blow of disendowment was not a lasting discouragement. It seemed to draw out a wonderful spirit of self-help; the weekly contributions of the negro flocks of a penny a week are regularly and willingly contributed, and amount to a large sum."[1]

The Presbyterian missions commenced by the Scottish Missionary Society in 1824 and by the Synod of the Secession Church in 1834 were united in 1847, and still retain an official connection with the United Presbyterian Church. They have, however, since 1866 supported all their own native ministers. They have also the whole responsibility of the schools, and they have been zealous in their labours for the extension of the Kingdom of Christ. Similarly the churches established by the London Missionary Society in British Guiana and

[1] Tucker, *English Church in other Lands*, p. 57.

in Jamaica have since 1867 been independent of the
funds and control of that society, receiving some limited
help for a time, but managing their own affairs and
providing for their own ministry. The Wesleyan Mission has also had a similar experience.

Not only has this been the case, but one of the first
results of emancipation was the awakening among the
Christian negroes of an eager and beautiful spirit of
anxiety for the well-being of their kith and kin in
Africa. "From the date of emancipation the churches"
(connected with the Baptist Missionary Society in
Jamaica) "have been eminently missionary churches in
the spirit they have exemplified, and in the efforts which
have been put forth. The African Mission of the parent
society was commenced in response to the earnest
appeal of the Jamaica Christians. At an early date
they formed a missionary society of their own."

As early as 1839 the Presbyterian churches in Jamaica
formed a missionary society to send the gospel to West
Africa. They received at the outset no encouragement
from the friends of the mission in Scotland, but they
persevered. In 1841 the Rev. Hope M. Waddell went
to Scotland from Jamaica to plead this new cause. The
outcome was the establishment of the deeply-interesting
and successful mission at Old Calabar on the coast of
West Africa in 1846.

"In 1851 the people belonging to the Episcopal
Church in Barbados founded an association for further-
ing the gospel in West Africa. The whole of the diocese took their part in the work, and the result has been
a very chivalrous mission to the Rio Pongas."[1]

The Bill for the renewal of the East India Company's
Charter in 1833 was also a veritable Emancipation Act,
the results of which were more important and more far-
reaching than can even now be fully estimated. The

[1] Tucker, *English Church in other Lands*, p. 59.

trade monopoly of the East India Company had been partially broken in 1813; in 1833 it was entirely swept away. The British Government compensated the stockholders for their losses on a liberal scale, and the company exchanged the functions of a great trading establishment for those more serious responsibilities which belong to a great government. Henceforth the Imperial Government took a direct and increasing responsibility for the administration of Indian affairs, and public opinion in Great Britain expressed itself freely on questions of Indian policy.

The East India Company's Charter, as renewed in 1813, had made an important change in the relation of the East India Company to education and religion by providing for an expenditure of £10,000 on education, and by making it possible to live and work in India without the company's licence. The establishment of the first bishopric was also then provided for. The two great missionary societies of the Church of England, together with the Society for the Propagation of Christian Knowledge, took an active part in the establishment of this episcopate, and contributed large sums towards the endowment of Bishop's College, Calcutta, thus linking the Indian episcopate with the mission cause from the outset. "All the bishops of Calcutta, though some more than others, have exhibited their interest in this work. They have been missionary bishops, and in their day and generation have been a spiritual power in the land. Who is there who does not thank God for the earnestness of Middleton, the devoutness of Heber, the practical sense and shrewdness of Wilson, the sweetness of Cotton?"[1]

The Bishopric of Calcutta comprised, until 1835, the whole of India, Ceylon, the Straits Settlements, and Australia! The new spirit manifested in the renewal of

[1] Sherring, *History of Protestant Missions in India*, p. 89.

the Charter in 1833 made it possible to alter this.   The
first Bishop of Madras was appointed in 1835.   The
Bishopric of Bombay was founded in 1837.   Since then
further subdivisions of territory and fresh appointments
have from time to time been made, as the extension of
Christian work connected with the Episcopal Church
has seemed to require increased episcopal supervision.
There are now no fewer than ten bishoprics in British
India, including Ceylon and Burmah.   Several of these
were established specially to meet the growing needs of
the native church.

The East India Company's Charter of 1833 was inspired by the broad and healthy spirit which was the
result of the first great Reform agitation in England.
It threw open the whole continent of India as a place of
residence for all subjects of His Majesty; it pronounced
the doom of slavery; it ordained that no native of British
territories in the East should, "by reason only of his
religion, place of birth, descent, or colour, be disabled
from holding any place, office, or employment".   It
also struck the last blow at the official connection of the
Government with idolatry.   What this meant may be
gathered from such accounts as that given by Dr.
Wilson of Bombay about his visit to Surat in 1835:—
"The English Government has still the responsibility,
and a fearful one it is, both for rulers and their agents,
of directly and publicly countenancing idolatry and
superstition.   The new moon, except during two months
in the year, is regularly saluted with five guns to please
the Mussulmans.   Rs.2000, I am told, are annually
contributed to the same people to assist them in the cele-
bration of their *eeds*.   The Chief of Surat and the British
Administrator of Justice in the province commits the
cocoa-nut to the river on the day of the great heathenish
procession at the break of the monsoon.   How all this
folly originated amidst the ungodliness of many of the

olden servants of the company, I can easily understand; but how it has been continued so long, I am puzzled to know."[1]

It required the resignation of his office by the Commander-in-chief of the Madras Army in 1837 because he would not sign an order to pay official respect to an idol, before public opinion was sufficiently roused to compel the company to carry out the provisions of the Bill.

From this time onward the development of missionary activity in India was immediate and rapid, and the success of missions, as shown even by the unsatisfactory and insufficient evidence of statistics, has been steadily increasing.

The development in the variety of agencies employed has not been less marked than the increase in the number of missionary organizations at work. In no part of the mission field has the missionary activity of the Church become so thoroughly systematized or exhibited so many-sided a breadth and scientific method as in India. Of the older societies which were at work in India anterior to the period under review, two only have to any material extent enlarged the field of their operations. The Society for the Propagation of the Gospel, whose work in India had previously been restricted almost entirely to the care of the old Danish Tranquebar Mission, has extended its operations very largely in South India, both in the Tamil and Telugu country. It has a strong and successful mission in Ahmednuggur, in the Bombay Presidency. Cawnpore and Delhi and the district around have been occupied since 1841 and 1852, and it has a deeply-interesting and successful mission in Chota Nagpore.

The Church Missionary Society has extended its work widely and on a larger scale. In South India it has

[1] Dr. G. Smith, *Life of Dr. John Wilson*, p. 187.

added to its Travancore and Tinnevelly Missions a large
and important mission in the Telugu country.   Its
missions in Western India have been well sustained.
In North India it has gone on from post to post
occupying a long line of important stations in the
North-west Provinces, the Punjaub, and even in Kashmir and on the borders of Afghanistan.   A remarkable
feature of this extension in North India is that so large
a part of it has been due to the earnest and generous
support of men in prominent positions in the public service, whose opportunities of judging of the results of
mission work have led them to desire the enlargement
of missionary operations.

The Baptist Missionary Society and the London Missionary Society have not attempted extension of the
area of work, though they have opened additional
stations in the field already occupied; in fact, the
London Missionary Society handed over its large and
promising mission in Gujarat to the Irish Presbyterians
in 1846 and 1860, and though it has since then undertaken a mission in Kumaon, this is not by any means so
large as what was relinquished in Gujarat.   Presbyterian
missions in India, which were represented at the beginning of this period by a very small but an exceptionally
able force in Bombay, Calcutta, and Madras, received a
great impetus by the various movements in the Presbyterian Churches in subsequent years.   At the Disruption
of the Church of Scotland in 1843, the whole of the
Indian staff of missionaries joined the Free Church, with
their native helpers and congregations, while the valuable educational and other buildings which had been
erected in the three centres remained the property of the
older mission.   The Free Church courageously accepted
the responsibility of providing new premises for the
mission work thus put into its hands, and also launched
out into a new mission at Nagpore in Central India.

The Church of Scotland sent out another set of missionaries in 1845 to occupy the premises vacated by the secession, and, after the Mutiny, commenced a mission in the Punjaub.   The Free Church has not sought extension of territory, but it has maintained its mission with a strength and vigour worthy of Wilson, Duff, Anderson, and Hislop, its great founders.

In 1840 the Irish Presbyterian Church was formed as a united body.   The first act of its Synod was to ordain missionaries for service in India.   At the suggestion of Dr. Wilson they undertook work in Gujarat, beginning at Katthiawar.   In 1846 the London Missionary Society transferred its mission in Surat to them, and subsequently (in 1859) it withdrew from the Mahi Kantha district in their favour.   This mission has been largely developed within the bounds of the district originally occupied.

In 1857, as the result of the Mutiny, the United Presbyterian Church determined to commence a mission in India.   Rajputana was chosen as the scene of its labours. The society now occupies five principal stations, with a strong staff of workers; medical, educational, and zenana work being equally prominent.

The Presbyterian Church of England has also confined itself to one district in India.   It commenced a mission at Rampore Bauleah in Bengal in 1876.

At the close of 1836 Madras was the only district occupied by the Wesleyan Missionary Society in India. Its work has very greatly developed since then.   In South India it has missions in Negapatam, Trichinopoly, the Mysore territory, and Hyderabad.   It commenced a mission at Calcutta in 1862, and at Lucknow in 1864.

The Welsh Calvinistic Methodists commenced a mission in Assam in 1841, and, confining themselves entirely to that region, they have built up a strong and successful work, partly among the Khasia and Jaintia Hills, and partly on the plains.

The Society of Friends sent their first missionary representative to India in 1866. In 1874 their work was definitely centred at Hoshangabad. Since then the mission has developed steadily in various forms of Christian effort, and its influence has spread in the Nerbudda Valley to other centres. Its educational work has been vigorously extended, and a most interesting and important experiment in the development of useful industries has been tried with encouraging results.

In 1882 Mr. F. Tucker, who had resigned his position in the Indian Civil Service in order to join the Salvation Army, was sent out to India to commence work in connection with the Army, which speedily established itself in a number of the principal centres of population.

This enumeration only touches the larger and more fully-organized missions. There are in addition a considerable number of missions which it is difficult to classify, and which represent individual ideas of duty. So vast, however, is the area of the country, and so great the population, that all these various organizations find abundant scope for their activities without interfering with each other, and there are still wide areas almost entirely untouched by Christian effort, notwithstanding the fact that American and Continental societies are also in the field in strong force.

The history of India during the period under review is divided into two very distinct parts by the great Mutiny of 1857. Into the familiar story of that dark hour, when the rule of Britain in India was shaken to its foundation, it is not necessary to enter. The nameless atrocities committed by the mutineers, the splendid heroism of our countrymen and countrywomen, and the staunch loyalty of a large body of the native troops, are things which have been graven deep in the memory of our nation. The Mutiny was a landmark in the progress of India never to be forgotten, and a point of change and new departure of profound importance. On November 1, 1858, a proclamation was issued which finally closed the long and remarkable history of the Imperial Company of Merchants and Traders, who had, in the pursuit of their own commercial ends, found themselves pushed on by the Unseen Hand to dominion over a continent. The exigencies of their position had brought out the splendid qualities of a large body of officials, and they had been fortunate in having as their chief administrators a succession of men of conspicuous ability and high character. But their policy had been throughout the greater part of the two centuries and a half unblushingly selfish. Only by the compulsion of public opinion in Britain had they, during the last few years of their rule, recognized that the peoples of the land they ruled had any relation to them other than that of being contributories towards their gain. The assumption of the Government of India by Her Majesty the Queen inaugurated a new era. Henceforward, duty towards India, the recognition of the tremendous responsibilities involved in the government of a great empire, became the predominant note of the new relation. Lord Dalhousie, the last governor-general before the Mutiny, had in many ways been a noble and worthy forerunner of the great change. Two things especially were begun by him which were fraught with incalculable blessing, and which, under Imperial rule, have been carried forward on a large scale. He introduced railways in 1851. Now there are upwards of 20,000 miles of railways completed in India, the economic value of which to the country, in promoting trade and intercommunication, and in making possible the conveyance of food in seasons of famine, has already been richly proved. Under his auspices also the famous education despatch of Sir Charles Wood was published in 1854, the sheet-anchor of the great system of elementary education which now prevails throughout India. The indirect effect of these two measures on the progress of missions has been very striking. The people of India have been caste-bound and custom-bound in a very marked degree, and ignorance, superstition, and shrinking from all change have been very painfully characteristic of their life. Facility of intercommunication enlarges knowledge of the world, and weakens the prejudice against new men and new ideas. The spread of education has stimulated the desire for knowledge, and has exerted a powerful influence on the position of woman. Men who had received education began to desire that their wives should also learn. Female education had been begun on a small scale in Calcutta more than thirty years before, and had been steadily pressed upon the people by every mission, but the total number of girls at school throughout India did not exceed 12,000. After the Mutiny female education made great advances. The Society for Promoting Female Education in the East was formed in 1834, and its first agent went to Calcutta in the following year, but its work was greatly restricted until after the Mutiny. The Scottish Ladies' Society for Female Education in India was established in 1837. The Indian Female Normal School Society began work also in Calcutta in 1852, where a Normal School was established in that year. In 1880 it was divided; the Church of England Zenana Society hived off, and the older portion took a new name. It is now known as the Zenana Bible and Medical Mission. Several of the older missionary societies encouraged the formation of special associations for women's work in connection with their more general operations; the earliest of these was the Wesleyan Missionary Ladies' Association, founded in 1859, "when the repugnance to female

education began to give way in the eastern mind, and
the wives of missionaries, instead of, as at first, finding
it difficult to obtain girls willing to be taught, had more
eager pupils than they could possibly instruct". Not
only have special associations for female work been
formed, but the missionary societies generally have
been compelled to recognize the necessity for appoint-
ing lady workers, and have sent out a steadily increasing number as the way has been opened.

Medical missions in India may be said to have begun
when Carey and his companion Dr. Thomas went out,
but since the Mutiny this branch of work has also been
very greatly extended. In 1874 the Mission to Lepers
in India was commenced, and has found a most neces-
sitous sphere of work among this large and greatly
afflicted class.

Statistics furnish a very imperfect means of estimat-
ing the extent and value of mission work, but even as
measured by statistics the progress of missions in India
has been remarkable. No effort was made to secure
general returns until 1851. From that date, however,
the statistics of all Protestant societies—British, American, and European—working in India have been tabu-
lated every decade with the following results:—

	1851.	1861.	1871.	1881.	1890.
Communicants	14,661	24,976	52,816	113,325	182,722
Scholars—Boys...	52,850	60,026	95,521	131,244	177,341
,, Girls...	11,193	15,969	26,611	56,408	102,375
Native Preachers, Ordained	21	97	225	461	797
,, Lay ...	493	1,266	1,985	2,488	3,491
Native Bible-women and ⎰ Zenana workers ... ⎱	—	—	837	1,643	3,278

Perhaps one of the most significant indications of
advance shown in the mission statistics is the growth of
work in the Zenanas. In 1871, 1300 houses were open

to the visits of the Zenana teachers; in 1890 the number had grown to 40,513.

These results have been achieved in spite of difficulty and opposition more formidable and more persistent than have been known in any other part of the world. The enormous mass of the population, second only to that of China, has rendered the task a herculean one. The number and the diversity of the languages spoken, amounting in all to about 150, has rendered co-operation, except within comparatively limited areas, impossible, and has required versions of the Scriptures as numerous and as unlike each other as those of all Europe. The amazing subtilty and the amazing power of the great religious system of Hinduism has made it the most formidable opponent Christianity has encountered in the heathen world. It includes almost the whole of the people within its pale, it has adapted itself to every stage of civilization and every phase of superstition. It has permeated the whole mass of Hindu society so effectually, that, like some powerful concrete, it has bound together every particle, every individual, in a common mass more impenetrable and harder than stone. By its elaborate system of a purely mechanical ritual, it has divorced religion from morality, and has silenced and drugged conscience by substituting ceremonial for moral conduct. Nowhere in all the world is there such abounding and bigoted religiousness coupled with such utter perversion of right and such utter deadening of the conscience.

Notwithstanding these great difficulties the converts have been gathered from every race and every caste and class. The Kols, the Gonds, the Santals, and other aboriginal tribes have been gathered by thousands into the Christian Church. The out-caste and low-caste people of Southern India and Travancore have found a new manhood and self-respect in the freedom of the gospel, and they have in tens of thousands placed themselves under Christian instruction. Though the number of conversions from among the higher castes and from the Mohammedans has been smaller on account of the far greater difficulties in their way, enough of striking instances of the conversion of Brahmans, and even of Mohammedan Moulvies, have been recorded to prove that among them also a very powerful influence has been exerted. Every society at work in India can point to mission centres, the story of which is an inspiration.

It is not so easy to estimate indirect and secondary results, because judgment is so liable to be influenced by prepossession and prejudice. There is some testimony, however, which may be regarded as beyond suspicion. A Report of the Secretary of State for India, presented to the House of Commons in 1892, says:—
"The various lessons which they inculcate have given to the people at large new ideas, not only on purely religious questions, but on the nature of evil, the obligations of law, and the motives by which human conduct should be regulated. Insensibly a higher standard of moral conduct is becoming familiar to the people, especially to the young, which has been set before them not merely by public teaching, but by the millions of printed books and tracts which are scattered widely through the country. This view of the general influence of their teaching, and of the greatness of the revolution which it is silently producing, is not taken by missionaries only. It has been accepted by many distinguished residents in India, and experienced officers of the Government."

Sir Charles Aitchison, late lieutenant-governor of the Punjaub, wrote in 1887:—
"Missionary teaching and Christian literature are leavening native opinion among the Hindus to an extent

quite startling to those who take a little personal trouble to investigate the facts. Missionaries have been the pioneers of education both vernacular and English; and they are still the only body who maintain schools for the low castes. To the missionaries we owe the movement in favour of female education; and the remarks in the last education report of the Punjaub show how efficient are the mission female schools, and how highly the labours of the missionaries are appreciated by the Government." [1]

Keshab Chandra Sen, the great leader of the Brahmo Samaj, viewed everything intellectual and religious from a very different standpoint from that occupied by Sir Charles Aitchison. Avowedly a Hindu, and the leader of a movement for the purification of Hinduism and the establishment of a new national religion on theistic and spiritual lines, he confessed continually that his inspiration came from Jesus Christ. On one occasion, addressing a great audience of his own countrymen, he said:

"As regards Christianity and its relation to the future Church of India, I have no doubt in my mind that it will exercise great influence on the growth and formation of that Church. The spirit of Christianity has already pervaded the whole atmosphere of Indian society, and we breathe, think, feel, and move in a Christian atmosphere. Native society is being raised, enlightened, and reformed under the influence of Christian education. If it is true that the future of a nation is determined by all the circumstances and agencies which to-day influence its nascent growth, surely the future Church of this country will be the result of the purer elements of the leading creeds of the day, harmonized, developed, and shaped under the influence of Christianity." [2]

---

[1] *American Baptist Missionary Herald*, May 1887.
[2] Lecture at Calcutta, January 23, 1869.

CEYLON is so closely connected with India that there has always been very much in common in the conditions of mission work.   It is, however, a Crown colony, and has been so since 1801, so that the attitude of the Government officials towards religious effort has never been marked by the jealous hostility which was so painfully characteristic of the East India Company in the early days of the century.   Buddhism has found one of its most sacred homes in Ceylon, and is professed by all true Singhalese, *i.e.* by fully two-thirds of the inhabitants.   Hinduism is the faith of the large population of Tamil and Malabar people who inhabit Jaffna and the northern part of the island, and also of the large number of coolies on the tea plantations, who mostly come from the districts of Travancore and Tinnevelly.   In addition to these two classes, who number about 2,750,000, there are also a small number of Veddahs, who seem to have been the aboriginal inhabitants of the island, and 200,000 Moormen, or men of Arab descent, who are Mohammedans, as are also the 10,000 Malays.   The Burghers, who are the descendants of the Portuguese and Dutch residents of former days, form a class quite apart from the others, and number about 18,000.

The Portuguese introduced Roman Catholicism into the island in the sixteenth century.   The Dutch who succeeded them made Catholicism penal.   They established chaplaincies and schools, and compelled people by thousands to profess Protestantism.   When Great Britain took the island, these coercive measures were stopped, and the people relapsed at once into a Buddhism which they had never really given up.   The first attempt at mission work among them was that of the London Missionary Society, which sent Dutch missionaries there in 1804.   The Baptists followed in 1812.   The first Wesleyan missionaries landed in 1814.   The Church Missionary Society commenced its mission in 1818.

The Society for the Propagation of the Gospel began work in 1838, and the Salvation Army landed in 1886.

The mission of the London Missionary Society consisted of *four* men, who from the first preached in Dutch as well as in Singhalese. All of them sooner or later severed their connection with the society, having settled as pastors of Dutch churches or engaged in general educational work under Government direction. The mission was closed in 1818.

The mission of the Baptist Society was commenced by the Rev. J. Chater, who is still remembered as the author of *A Singhalese Grammar*, and as the founder of many churches and prosperous schools and also of a native press. The mission has been maintained with vigour ever since, having three important centres of work, at Colombo, Kandy, and Ratnapore. A large number of the congregations gathered by the mission in these districts have already become self-supporting and independent.

The friendly attitude of the Government of Ceylon towards missions was marked in the experience of the Wesleyans when they landed at Galle in 1814. The Governor received the missionaries with great kindness, entertained them at Government House, and offered them subsidies for any schools they might commence. They decided to begin work at once among the Tamil-speaking people in Northern Ceylon and the Singhalese in the south. Jaffna and Batticaloa were made the centres of their Tamil work, while Galle and Matura were chosen for work among the native Singhalese. The mission has greatly prospered in every branch, a large number of schools are maintained, including two colleges, which stand high among the educational establishments of the island. There is a book-room and printing-press at Colombo, which is a very important auxiliary to the mission.   Medical work is also being done in the northern district.

The Church Missionary Society has followed very similar lines to the other societies.   It commenced work among the Tamil people and also the Singhalese. Nellore, near Jaffna, Cotta, near Colombo, and Kandy, became its chief centres.   At Kandy, in addition to work among the Singhalese, it has the head-quarters of a large and successful work among the Tamil coolies on the tea estates.   In connection with its Jaffna Mission is a native evangelical society, which is managed entirely by the native Christians, and sends its catechists to visit a scattered and needy population in the jungles to the south.

The Society for the Propagation of the Gospel has been the representative of the more distinctively ecclesiastical side of Christian work in Ceylon.   It took an active part in the establishment of the bishopric, and, to quote the words of the bishop : " If I am to sum up the results of the society's work in Ceylon, I should say: the society has given a missionary character to all the Church's work here.   It has supplied a missionary side to the work of almost every chaplain and catechist."

Caste, which is so radical and so powerful a factor in Hinduism on the continent of India, has little influence in Ceylon, where almost all the Hindu population are of very low caste.   Buddhism knows nothing of it, and of course the Mohammedans do not recognize it.   The chief difficulty in mission work has arisen from the spiritual lethargy induced by Buddhism, and by the gross ignorance and superstition to which its followers have sunk by the loss of all its nobler features, and its deterioration into a system of devil-worship and magic.

Education has been a prominent and very successful feature in the work of each of the missionary societies, and the development of the native character and ministry has received much attention.

The spirit of missionary enterprise having turned to the great East, has not been content with attempting great things for God, to use the language of Carey, but has with true appreciation of duty and splendid enthusiasm regarded no opportunity as too unimportant, and no sphere too small for its energies. On the eastern side of the Bay of Bengal is BURMAH, the whole of which is now politically included in the Indian Empire. It is, however, inhabited by races differing from any of those who are found in British India, and their religion is entirely different. Buddhism, modified to some extent by aboriginal superstitions, is the religion of six-sevenths of the population, and has, in its own sluggish way, a surprising hold upon them. "The women are more devout Buddhists than the men, and science, art, and knowledge are all saturated with Buddhism, the one bond of national life." The maintenance of Buddhism becomes a family matter, for there are upwards of 18,000 priests and an enormous company of "unbeneficed clergy, the junior members of the order of the Yellow Robe, who daily go forth with the mendicant's bowl, and help in the routine of the monastery under their house superior".

Burmah has been best known in missionary annals from the wonderful story of the Karen Mission carried on by the American Baptists, and associated with the life and labours of Dr. Judson. British missionary effort has been represented since 1859 by the Society for the Propagation of the Gospel. It commenced its mission in response to the appeal and effort of local chaplains, and has gradually extended its work through both Lower and Upper Burmah, having stations at Moulmein, Rangoon, Tounghoo, Akyab, many villages in the valley of the Irrawaddy, Mandalay, Shwebo, and

Pyinmana. It also includes within its sphere the degraded aborigines of the Andaman Islands and the Malay Nicobarese. The educational work of the missionaries first gave them an influence with the Burmese and helped them greatly in extending their mission. The story of the establishment of the mission at Mandalay, and of the connection of Mr. Marks with the notorious King Theebaw, is full of interest. A mission among the Karens was commenced in 1875, and has resulted in a large ingathering of converts.

The kingdom of Siam, and the great islands of Sumatra and Java and also Dutch Borneo, are scarcely touched by British missions, being now left almost entirely to the energies of American and continental societies. The British possessions in the Malay Peninsula have been the scene of British missionary effort from the early years of the century. Malacca, which was in those days one of the most important, as it was one of the oldest, European settlements in the East, was the home of a strong and thriving mission of the London Missionary Society from 1815 to 1843, and on account of its facilities of trade communication with China, became the centre of those educational and literary efforts to reach the Chinese which filled the long years of waiting before China was opened. Penang and Singapore were also stations of the same society during that period. The Society for the Propagation of the Gospel is now the chief representative of missionary effort in various parts of the Peninsula. Its work is done here, as in many other places, with the co-operation of local chaplains and churchmen, as it was commenced in response to local appeal. The mission is not an easy one, for the population is of a peculiarly mixed character. Large tracts of country are occupied by Europeans in the cultivation of sugar and spices, the labour required for working the estates being obtained by the importation of coolies from South India and from various parts of China. The diversities of tongue among these immigrants are so great as to cause constant perplexity. At Singapore, for instance, it is reported that "on Sundays services are held in Chinese, Tamil, and Malay. There are so many dialects, or rather languages, spoken by the different Chinese who come to the Straits, that there is considerable difficulty in making the service intelligible to the mixed congregation which attends it. It is partially met by the prayers being said in one dialect, the lessons read in two others, while the sermon is preached in Ho Kien, and rendered by the catechist into Cantonese." [1]

The mission was begun in Singapore in 1861, taking up work which had been commenced by the chaplain and a local committee in 1857. Catechists are also maintained at Malacca and Penang under the direction of the local chaplains. A European missionary is maintained among the people on the estates in Province Wellesley, the funds for his support being largely provided by local generosity.

The English Presbyterian Church commenced a mission in Singapore in 1881, and have prosecuted it with vigour and considerable success. They, in common with the Society for the Propagation of the Gospel, find the babel of tongues and the constantly shifting character of the population great hindrances to work. Both missions are paying great attention to education.

The large island of Borneo has since 1848 been the scene of a deeply-interesting mission. It was begun at the instance of Rajah Brooke of Sarawak, by a committee who obtained contributions for the "Borneo Church Mission Fund", and was taken over by the Society for the Propagation of the Gospel, in 1853.

[1] *Digest of S.P.G. Records*, pp. 697-98.

The first step taken by the society was to promote the establishment of a bishopric.   In 1855 the Bishop of Labuan was appointed.   The climate is very trying, the Dyak tribes are by nature fierce, piratical, and extremely superstitious barbarians, the large Mohammedan population is intensely fanatical, and the political history of Sarawak was for many years very chequered; but the mission has steadily progressed in spite of all these difficulties, and is now established at eight principal centres.   In 1882 a commencement was made of work in North Borneo among tribes who have a large admixture of Chinese blood.

It is not easy to realize to-day what was the relation of CHINA to the western world at the beginning of the Queen's reign.   To-day foreigners have the right to travel, to trade, to settle, and to acquire and hold property in any part of the eighteen provinces of the empire.   Doubtless the right cannot always be exercised with freedom or safety, but that is due to the deep - rooted character of local prejudice against foreigners which still exists in many parts of China. Foreign traders are, however, settled in not a few important centres even as far west as Chung King, 1400 miles up the course of the Yangtsze river, and European and American missionaries are scattered everywhere, even in remote places in the provinces farthest from the coast.   In 1837 China was absolutely closed to the foreigner.   There was only a single port in which he was allowed to trade, and even then only under humiliating conditions in which he suffered much from the caprice or the exactions of the local authorities.   There was not a place except Canton where he could secure a house to dwell in, and at Canton he was confined within a limited area and was not allowed to go about.   The arrogance of the Chinese and their contemptuous and insolent treatment of foreigners made communication with them in the early part of the century exceedingly difficult. Even the great East India Company could only communicate with the local authorities at Canton by humble petition presented through the Hong of Chinese merchants.

Mission work under such conditions was almost impossible. There is no more interesting or suggestive picture in mission history than that of Robert Morrison toiling on year after year in Canton at his great literary tasks, translating the whole Bible, preparing a lexicon, writing books and tracts in expectation of a time when they should be required. He was unable to go beyond the precincts of the East India Company's factory; he was not allowed to preach among the Chinese, yet he laboured from 1808 to 1834, patient, indomitable, faithful, gathering round him the Chinese servants and others connected with the factory and speaking to them of Christ. Six years after he went to China, William Milne, a man of kindred spirit, joined him, but Milne was not allowed to live in Canton. He therefore went to Malacca, and there established an Anglo-Chinese College, and set up a printing-press, from which millions of pages of printed statements and appeals in Chinese were poured forth and found their way into the closed empire, and even, it is said, reached the Imperial court in Peking. One of Morrison's first converts, Liang-a-fa, became also the first ordained Chinese preacher, and was the writer of a tract, "The True Principle of the World's Salvation", which to this day is being circulated largely in China, and has had a remarkable history. Other missionaries joined the two great pioneers, and patiently waited and worked at Malacca and Singapore, acquiring a knowledge of the language, issuing Christian literature, and expecting until the way should be opened for their advance into China. Milne died in 1822, Morrison followed him in

1834, but the gates were still closed and barred, apparently with more determination than ever.   In 1835 Mr. Medhurst, at the request of the directors of the London Missionary Society, undertook a trip up the Chinese coast.   He and an American missionary, the Rev. Edwin Stevens, went as far north as the Shantung Promontory, visiting Shanghai, Che Kiang, and Fo Kien.   Their experiences were on the whole pleasant, but gave little hope of any permanent access to the country.   "The mandarins told me repeatedly that the orders from the Government were always to treat strangers with politeness and to supply them with necessaries at the public expense, but to get them away as soon as possible. . . .   I think it entirely out of the question for a missionary to think of taking up his residence in any part of China except Canton, or to penetrate into the interior by roads or rivers; indeed I question whether he would be allowed to remain on shore more than a few days without molestation."

The result of this journey, when it had been reported to Peking, was an Imperial edict issued to the Governor of Canton, and threatening, "if they again indulge their own desires and act thus irregularly, they (*i.e.* all the foreigners) must be immediately driven out of the port and no longer allowed commercial intercourse ".[1]

The hostility of the authorities was vented upon all who were in any way associated with the foreigners. Five or six Chinamen in Canton who had learned the gospel from Morrison had the courage to make known that they were Christians, and they were made to suffer.   In the report of the London Missionary Society for 1837 it is recorded that "the persecution of the native Christians at Canton had been relentlessly pursued by the incensed functionaries of the native Govern-

[1] *L.M.S. Report,* 1836, pp. 24, 25.

ment ". Yet at this very time a great political change
in another part of the world was destined to be the
means of doing what had been hoped for in vain for
more than a century. The renewal of the East India
Company's Charter in 1833, which was the cause of
such wide-spread and radical changes in India, became,
though no one could have foreseen it at the time, the
beginning of the modern history of China. One very
important feature in that great legislative measure was
the abolition of the company's monopoly in British
trade with China. The East India Company henceforth
ceased to be direct traders, but private enterprise was
eager to take their place notwithstanding all the dis-
abilities and annoyances to which the traders were
exposed. The Government of Great Britain, having
thrown open the trade, necessarily assumed towards
all such traders the position of protector, and became
involved in their difficulties and quarrels. Among the
articles of the trade which the East India Company had
carried on with China was opium. At first the amount
required and imported was very small. In 1767 it
amounted to 200 chests. But the taste for it among
the Chinese had steadily and largely grown until the
amount annually imported had reached 70,000 or 80,000
chests. The opium was grown in India, and the profits
on its sale were so great that when the life of the company as a great trading corporation ended in 1833, and
they became a great ruling body, the cultivation of
opium was retained in the hands of the Government
for the sake of the revenue it yielded, and it was sold
periodically to the traders, who exported it to China.
Meanwhile the Chinese Government had awaked to the
mischievous character of the drug which was thus being
poured into the country. First they protested against
it, then they forbade it. But the trade paid too well
to be given up, and opium-smuggling became one of

the most exciting and lucrative employments in the
East. It was to the financial interest of the Government
of India to support and encourage the traders, and the
moral questions involved in stimulating and forcing on
this traffic seem not to have been thought of. Great
Britain was a consenting party to the fiscal arrangements of the company, and, alas! when India finally
came directly under Imperial rule in 1858, the opium
monopoly was again left untouched as one of the chief
sources of state revenue.

The war between England and China which commenced in 1830 has been commonly known as the
"first opium war". Doubtless this is not quite a
fair, or at least an exhaustive, description of the causes
of the war. There were many old scores to be settled.
Two embassies had been sent to China, the first in 1795
and the second in 1816, to represent to the emperor the
exceedingly unsatisfactory position of foreign merchants.
Both these embassies had entirely failed in obtaining any
improvement, and the arrogance and exactions of the
Chinese had greatly increased. There was, therefore,
very great tension of feeling, which only required an
exciting cause to produce strife. This exciting cause
came in the seizure and destruction by the Chinese
authorities of upwards of 20,000 chests of opium stored
in Canton. This was done with the sanction of the
British superintendent of trade, but was promptly resented by the British Government, and as no compensation was given to the merchants, war was declared. The
war was ended by the treaty of Nan King (August 29,
1842), by which Hong Kong was ceded to Great Britain
in perpetuity, and the right of residence was granted to
foreigners in Canton, Amoy, Fu Chow, Ningpo, and
Shanghai. "Two years later, France and America con-
cluded treaties with China, which included the right to
erect places of worship in the treaty ports. The French

treaty led the way in procuring the revocation of the persecuting edicts of 1724 and later, and the issue of a decree of toleration."

The whole history of the opium traffic in China is extremely sad and humiliating. There is no evidence that it was known as an article of common consumption until it was introduced from India. Its use was stimulated by the Company of British Merchants for their own gain. It was made contraband by the Chinese, and remained so even after the war of 1839, and until the war of 1857. After that war, it was admitted under heavy duties. Then the Chinese Government sanctioned the cultivation of the poppy by their own people. Now extensive districts of the most fertile land in China are given up to the growth of the drug, and the import of opium from India has been seriously affected by the large quantities of the home-grown article which are on the market. The testimony of those who since that day have become intimately acquainted with the inner life of China and the Chinese is practically unanimous as to the wide-spread and appalling nature of the evils introduced to China by the habit of opium-smoking. The medical missionaries in China of every Church and of every western nation say, "it is difficult to speak too strongly of the physical and moral evil and of the social misery which is being wrought in China by the wide-spread and increasing indulgence in the use of opium". Experienced clerical missionaries, men who have had large opportunity for coming into close contact with the people, and men who are not given to exaggerate, are equally emphatic. The Rev. J. G. Kerr, M.D., a missionary of more than forty years' experience in China, gives the following testimony: "The crowning evil of all is in the deterioration of the moral faculty. The moral sense becomes blunted, regard for truth is lost, and the victim loses that sense of honour and regard for right which is the basis of all nobility of character. The fact remains that the opium habit destroys the moral sense, and the evidence of it is found in the fact that missionaries with one consent refuse to admit opium-smokers into the Christian Church without previous reformation."

The effect of the opium traffic as a hindrance to missionary effort can scarcely be exaggerated. It has been forced upon China by the arms of the nation which has been foremost in sending the Christian preacher. The Chinese exclusiveness and dislike of foreigners has been intensified to positive hatred. Intelligent and patriotic Chinamen have continually made their objection to the gospel, that the "foreign barbarians" have forced themselves into their country against their will with their religion in one hand and this most pestilent poison in the other. Unfortunately the consideration of the large amount of revenue provided for the needs of the Indian Government by the sale of opium, and which has amounted since the commencement of the Queen's reign to the enormous sum of £238,000,000, has been allowed to stifle the great questions of public morality which are involved in the traffic. This revenue has been obtained, not simply by taxing an article of general consumption, but by the actual growth and manufacture of opium by the Government, China being compelled by force to admit it to her people. The Government has become thus directly responsible for the traffic and for all the moral evils which have followed in its train.

Unpropitious as were the circumstances under which the gates of China were opened, and though the permission to reside in the treaty ports required that the foreigner should not make any journey outside their precincts which was not accomplished within twenty-four hours, the missionary societies were prompt to recognize the significance of the fact that the day of their opportunity had arrived.   Every one of the five ports was speedily occupied by the London Missionary Society, the Church Missionary Society, the missions of the English Presbyterian Church, and the Wesleyans; and missions commenced then in much limitation and much difficulty have all become strong centres of active, self-reliant, and prosperous work.

The Chinese speedily gave numberless evidences that they had no intention of keeping the treaty if they could avoid it, while the foreign traders showed that they were equally determined to press on at all risk.   Friction was constantly arising in connection with the open and organized contraband trade in opium.   At length the alleged insult to the British flag in connection with the capture of the lorcha *Arrow* led to a second war, which commenced in 1857 by the taking of Canton, and was terminated in 1860 by the occupation of Peking.   This great struggle against Chinese obstinacy and treachery had even more important results than the previous war.

" Henceforth the aspect of China began to be changed. The middle wall of partition which had so long separated as a horizon between her and foreign nations was swept away, her exclusiveness was penetrated, her isolation uncovered, her supercilious bearing rebuked, the high prerogatives she had assumed were abased, and the hitherto peerless ' Son of Heaven ' found himself face to face with a new set of conditions . . . by a treaty which confirmed (1) to commerce and missions the right of unmolested access to his dominions, (2) to ministers plenipotentiary the right of residence in his capital, and (3) to all, the immunities of an extra-territorial jurisdiction."[1]

This treaty contained a very important clause providing for the protection of all who propagated or who adopted Christianity.   The additional right of *residence*

[1] Dr. J. Y. Allen at Shanghai Conference, 1890.

in any part of China, and to purchase as well as to rent land and buildings, was also ultimately obtained for all missionaries through the insertion of it in the French treaty on behalf of the missionaries of the Roman Catholic Church.

The freedom accorded by treaty was not recognized in general practice for many years. Missionary journeys were undertaken often at serious peril to life and limb. Attempts to obtain a lodgment in the cities by the purchase of property were defeated by the hostility of the authorities and the violence of the mob. One province was practically closed to all foreigners until 1897. None the less, the right to live and work without restriction, having been conceded, was at once accepted with a great outburst of missionary zeal. The additional ports opened by the treaty were first occupied, and then missions began to spread in many directions. The four societies which had represented British Christian zeal in China before the war, have become sixteen, in addition to the British and Foreign Bible Society and the National Bible Society of Scotland, and every one of the eighteen provinces has become the scene of wide-spread and varied labours.

The first missionary organization to enter the country when it was opened was naturally the London Missionary Society. In 1843 it transferred its printing-press from Malacca to the new British colony of Hong Kong, and established an Anglo-Chinese Theological Seminary instead of the Anglo-Chinese College which had been maintained at Malacca since 1818. The Rev. Dr. Legge, who had joined the Malacca Mission in 1839, became the first missionary at Hong Kong, and during the next thirty-four years was largely instrumental in building up a vigorous native Christian Church in that colony. He also gained for himself a reputation as a Sinologue by his translation of the *Chinese Classics*, and in 1876 was appointed Professor of Chinese in the University of Oxford.

In the same year (1843) the same society entered upon work at Shanghai, and Dr. Lockhart established the first hospital in China. In the year following Amoy was occupied, and in 1847 a medical mission was commenced in Canton, and Dr. Hobson laboured with much success until 1856, when his work was closed in consequence of the troubles which preceded the outbreak of war with China. He had meanwhile published works in Chinese on anatomy, surgery, medicine, and midwifery, which have proved of very great value. In 1861 the Revs. Griffith John and Robert Wilson commenced a mission at Hankow which has been since then a remarkable centre of wide-spread influence, and has now become one of a cluster of stations, of which the others are Wu Chang, Hiao Kan, and King Shan. In 1888 the Mission in Central China was further extended by the commencement of work in Chung King, the commercial capital of the western province of Sze Chuen. In 1897 a further step was made possible by the opening to foreigners of the province of Hunan. The year that saw the commencement of the Central China Mission saw also the opening of North China to missionary effort. Dr. Edkins commenced a mission in Tientsin in 1861. In the following year Dr. Lockhart, having been appointed physician to the new British Legation at Peking, was able to obtain premises in the capital, which would not have been allowed on any other condition, and opened a mission hospital; Dr. Edkins joining him to commence the Peking Mission. In 1870 James Gilmour commenced his truly apostolic labours and journeys among the Mongols, which, after sixteen years, were terminated by settlement at Chao Yang, in Southern Mongolia. The North China Mission was expanded by the establishment of new centres of European work at Chi Chou, Yen San (or T'sang Chou), and Tung An.

The Church Missionary Society was not far behind the London Missionary Society in taking advantage of the openings made by the treaty. Already, in 1837, the Rev. G. B. Squire had been sent out to commence a tentative mission at Singapore and Macao. In 1844 the Revs. G. Smith and T. M'Clatchie arrived to open work on the mainland, and a mission was commenced at Shanghai. Four years after (1848), on the advice of Mr. M'Clatchie, the society entered Ningpo, and in 1850 they occupied Foochow. Both of these missions have been fortunate in enjoying the services of men of exceptional ability. The Rev. G. E. Moule, afterwards Bishop of Mid China, and his brother, the Rev. A. E. Moule, the Archdeacon of Shanghai, were both at Ningpo as missionaries.

The workers at Foochow laboured for eleven years without a convert. Yet that mission now extends over seventeen counties, and numbers more than 11,000 adherents. The educational work carried on is extensive and complete, comprising a large number of elementary schools, several boarding-schools for girls, and others for boys, a higher grade school, with which is now associated classes for thorough medical training of men and also of women, and a theological training college with a large number of students. There are also two mission hospitals and a home for lepers.

The Rev. G. Smith, one of the two pioneer missionaries, became the first Bishop of Hong Kong. As the result of an urgent appeal from him for help in meeting the spiritual needs of the Chinese population of the colony, a mission was commenced in Hong Kong in 1861, the first two pastors of the native Church which was gathered there being Chinamen who had become Christians and received their education in Australia.

In 1862 the Rev. J. S. Burdon, afterwards Bishop of Hong Kong, commenced a mission in Peking. This was transferred to the Society for the Propagation of the Gospel in 1880, and the Church Missionary Society confined itself thereafter entirely to Central and South China. A mission in Canton was opened in 1882, and Pakhoi was occupied in 1886. The latest development of work connected with the Church Missionary Society is the lay mission in Sze Chuen under the leadership of the Rev. J. Horsburgh.

In 1845 the Synod of the English Presbyterian Church decided to commence a mission in China. For two years they made it a subject of special prayer, and sought for someone who would be suitable to be the leader in the new enterprise. " None appearing, the Committee had actually agreed to recommend the Synod in 1847 to abandon China and turn to India instead, when, to the surprise and delight of the Committee, the Rev. W. C. Burns presented himself at the Synod, and on the Convener asking him how soon he could go out, he replied with characteristic readiness, and pointing to a carpet bag, 'To-morrow'." Mr. Burns had been specially prepared for great service. He was a "son of the manse", was educated for the ministry, was endowed with a vigorous understanding, a voice of great compass and power, strong conviction, boundless energy, burning ardour, and a soul possessed in an unusual degree by the sense of union with Christ. From 1839, when he began regular ministry in Scotland, a remarkable spiritual power was exerted by him. He was the centre of that great spiritual movement known as the Kilsyth revival, which spread through so large a part of Scotland from 1839 to 1841. From 1841 to 1844 he was engaged in evangelistic work in the north of England, and then went to Canada, where his preaching exerted the same attractive and quickening power as had been

associated with it in Scotland and England. He went
to China in the same spirit, and from the first became a
great power.   For two years he lived at Hong Kong,
learning the Chinese language and ministering to the
small community of his countrymen.   One result of his
brief ministry was that one of his hearers, Dr. Young,
decided to give himself to mission work, and in 1850
went to Amoy, where he commenced a mission and was
warmly welcomed by the missionaries connected with
the American Presbyterians and the London Missionary
Society, who had already been labouring there for some
years.   Mr. Burns had in the meantime been to Canton,
where he remained for sixteen months, but failing to
secure premises for mission work, he joined Dr.
Young at Amoy in 1851, and commenced what from the
outset proved a mission greatly blessed of God.   The
people of the Fokien province are a sturdy and energetic
race, vigorous in opposition, and equally vigorous and
independent when they become Christians.   The three
missions which have Amoy as their centre have all had
sad, sad experience of the power of the Chinese in opposition, but they have also all had remarkable success.
There is no part of China where the principle of self-
support has been so generally and so heartily recognized,
or where the Christians have exhibited more earnestness
or determination in spreading the gospel.

In 1856 Mr. Burns visited Swatow, and was the means
of commencing in that important city and crowded district a second mission of the Presbyterian Church, which
in its subsequent extension and success has rivalled that
at Amoy.   Next we find him visiting Foochow, and
preaching for several months in that district.   In 1863
he went to Peking in the hope that he might procure,
through the intervention of Her Majesty's representative,
for native Protestant Christians the privilege of ex-
emption from the duty of supporting idolatry and the

ancestral worship, which had been obtained by the French Government for the Roman Catholics the year before. He remained four years in Peking, preaching and writing with his accustomed energy. Then he went on to New Chwang, the great seaport of Manchuria, and commenced a mission there. In this place he ended his remarkable career on April 8, 1868.

The English Presbyterian Church commenced in 1860 a third important mission by sending Messrs. Douglas and Mackenzie to the island of Formosa.

The Wesleyan Missionary Society were the next to enter China. They began, through the energy and devotion of the Rev. G. Piercy, a mission in Canton in 1852. Ten years later their mission was extended to Hankow and Wu Chang, and rapidly extended in the province of Hupeh. Their medical mission in Hankow was the first in Central China. In 1885, under the inspiration of the Rev. David Hill, a Wesleyan Lay Mission for Central China was established, and an earnest band of men known as the "Joyful News Mission" were sent out to carry on the work of evangelization.

After the treaty of Tientsin in 1858, other societies in rapid succession followed the pioneers. The Methodist New Connexion sent out two missionaries, who reached Tientsin in 1860. That great city has since been the centre of a very varied work which has extended far in North Shantung, and also in the district to the north of Tientsin. The United Methodist Free Churches chose Ningpo as their field of labour in 1864, and have confined themselves to that district and the district around Wenchow.

The Baptist Missionary Society accepted the services of Messrs. Kloekers and Hall, both of whom had been labouring in China long enough to have acquired a knowledge of the language, and commenced a mission in 1862. The missionaries went first to Shanghai. In the following year they removed to Chefoo, and that city was the centre of work until 1875, when it was finally abandoned for an inland station, Tsing Chow Foo. The Shantung province has continued to be the chief scene of the work of the mission. The great plain formed by the Yangtsze and the Yellow River, and traversed by them, is of enormous extent, densely populated, and constantly the scene of wide-spread trouble as the result of floods or of droughts. The great famine of 1876–77 in Shantung, when several millions perished, was the means of commending the mission to the people, and great blessings followed. The work was extended to the province of Shansi in 1877, and more recently to the far western province of Shensi,—a province which has peculiar interest from the fact that the Nestorians were there 1100 years ago, as shown by the great Tablet of Si Ngan Fu.

In 1868 the Irish Presbyterian Church took up the mission at New Chwang, Manchuria, which had been commenced by William Burns. It was followed by the United Presbyterian Church of Scotland in 1872, who began work at Moukden, the capital of Manchuria. The Established Presbyterian Church of Scotland chose a sphere in the Yangtsze Valley, and in 1877 began its mission at I'Chang, nearly 1000 miles up the river. The latest British Missionary Society to undertake work in China is the Friends' Foreign Mission Association, one of whose members settled in Hankow in 1884. In 1890 the mission was settled at Chung King in the province of Sze Chuen.

The most remarkable manifestation of Christian zeal for the conversion of China is in the history of the organization founded by Dr. Hudson Taylor in 1865, and which has become well known throughout Christendom as the China Inland Mission. Mr. Taylor was the

son of a devoted evangelist at Barnsley in Yorkshire,
where he was born in 1832. As a youth of sixteen he
became by God's grace an earnest and devout Christian. His father was deeply interested in the progress
of the gospel in other lands, and though prevented
himself from going abroad, had been led to pray that, if
God gave him a son, he might devote his life to the
evangelization of China. When the youth became converted, his father's prayers began to find immediate
answer in the awakening of a strong desire to be a missionary. The reading of Medhurst's *China* led him to
see the value of medical missions, while deep conviction
that he was called of God to this special service made
him use all the means in his power to fit himself in body
as well as mind for the work. During the course of his
preparatory studies—first as assistant to a doctor connected with the Hull School of Medicine, and who was
also surgeon in a number of factories, and afterwards in
London—he was brought, by some very striking and
impressive personal experiences, to a deep realization of
the power and of the true meaning of a life of faith as a
life of real dependence on the personal guidance and
personal provision of God. He went out to China as
the first representative of the China Evangelization
Society, arriving in Shanghai on March 1, 1854. It
was an exciting and troubled time; the native city was,
and had for some months been, in the hands of a body
of Cantonese rebels known as the "Red Turbans". He
lived for six months with Dr. Lockhart of the London Missionary Society while commencing his studies
in the language, and subsequently, after the rebels had
been expelled, he found a lodging in the native city,
enduring hardness from the first in consequence of his
very limited means and the high price of everything.
Early in 1856 a godly sea-captain offered him and Mr.
Burns a passage to Swatow if they would go down and

commence a mission there. Gladly accepting the invitation, the two evangelists went, and Hudson Taylor's medical knowledge was the means of gaining the friendship of a mandarin. Through him what appeared at first to be the insuperable difficulty of obtaining a place to live in among a notoriously wild and lawless population was overcome, and the mission of the English Presbyterian Church was commenced. It was necessary for Mr. Taylor to return to Shanghai, and circumstances quite beyond his control prevented him from going back to Swatow. He went instead to Ningpo, and remained there three years. During this time he married, and here also he took the bold step of resigning his connection with the Chinese Evangelization Society, and cast himself entirely upon the care of God. In 1860 it was necessary for him to return to England on account of the state of his health. The time, however, was not lost, though he stayed in England five years. In addition to inducing five others to go out to work at Ningpo, he prepared for the press an edition of the New Testament in the romanized colloquial of Ningpo, and while studying the Scriptures for this purpose the idea which took shape in the formation of the China Inland Mission laid hold of him.

"In undertaking this work", he writes, "I, in my short-sightedness, saw nothing beyond the use that the book, with its marginal references, would be to the native Christians of Ningpo, but I have often realized since then that without those months of feeding and feasting on the Word of God I should have been quite unprepared to form on its present basis a mission such as the China Inland Mission.

"In the study of that divine Word, I learned that to obtain successful workers, not elaborate appeals for help, but, first, earnest prayer to *God* to thrust forth labourers, and secondly, the deepening of the spiritual life of the Church, so that men should be unable to stay at home, were what was needed. I saw that the apostolic plan was not to be concerned about ways and means, but to go and do the work, trusting in His sure word who has said, ' Seek ye first the kingdom of God and His righteousness, and all these things shall be added unto you'.

" It was decided, in the first place, to form the new association upon a broadly catholic basis, inviting the sympathy and co-operation of all the Lord's people, irrespective of denominational differences. By this means it was hoped to avoid the danger of drawing upon the resources of any one special body of Christians, either for men or means, and to raise a testimony also to the essential unity of the Church of Christ, in which there are diversities of operations, but it is the same God that worketh all in all.

" Then, as regards the fellow-labourers to be sought and accepted in connection with the work, the supreme importance of *spiritual* qualifications, rather than intellectual, social, or any other, was from the first distinctly recognized.

" And in the third place, the difficulty as to a possible deflection of *funds* from old-established channels was met by a very simple but radical change in the ordinary method of obtaining an income for the support of missionary work. To begin with, it was decided, once and for all, never to go into debt. The funds received would be used as they were needed, but beyond this not one penny more. And as a natural outcome of such an understanding, no regular salaries could be promised to the workers."[1]

The mission commenced under such conditions has been wonderfully blessed. Its workers have shown conspicuous courage and devotion, and have pene-

[1] *Story of the China Inland Mission*, i., pp. 195, 233, 34, 35.

trated to the remotest parts of China. It has missionaries in every one of the eighteen provinces, and permanent centres of work in fourteen. Even Thibet, the only absolutely closed and apparently hopeless country in the East, is being pertinaciously assailed by the enterprise of its pioneers. The movement has now become international as well as interdenominational, associated bodies of workers from Canada and Australia, Sweden, Norway, and the United States of America having joined their ranks.

China as a field for missionary effort has presented some unique features alike on the side of advantage and of difficulty. Nowhere else in the world is there so vast a population practically homogeneous. With the exception of the Tartar rulers in the north, they are practically one race, and their language is one. There are difficulties of pronunciation and dialectic differences which make the men of one province quite unintelligible in other parts of China, and there are a number of local colloquial tongues, especially in South China; but the written character is available and is understood equally well by educated men in every part of the Chinese Empire, and even in Japan. Moreover, though it is evidently a mistake to suppose that the people as a whole are educated, because it is probable that not more than one in ten can read, yet there is a percentage of readers everywhere, and the people as a whole have a profound respect for education and for literature. In consequence of this, literature has been a great power in missionary effort, and has been very extensively used by all missionary societies. On the other hand, Western education, which has proved so great a force of disintegration and preparation in British India, has until quite recently been almost useless as a missionary agency in China, and has had no attraction for the people at large. Education on native lines,

which consists entirely in acquiring by memory a knowledge of the native classics, and in preparing, on certain
lines prescribed by ancient custom, theses based upon
them, has been the only avenue to preferment and
honour.   There has therefore been no inducement from
self-interest to acquire any Western knowledge, even on
the most elementary subjects, except in the very limited
sphere of connection with foreign business houses in
the treaty ports; while the overweening conceit of the
Chinese has led them to despise the knowledge prized
by Western nations, and about which they are, as a
nation, profoundly ignorant.   Since the recent war with
Japan there has been a great awakening, and from
every great centre of Chinese life there now comes an
eager demand for the establishment of schools in which
the English language and Western science may be
taught.

The strange fatuity with which an intelligent, capable,
and eminently practical people like the Chinese have
allowed themselves to be bound hand and foot with the
grave clothes of ancient usage and reverence for the
teachings of the sages of bygone times shows itself in
every direction, and in nothing more injuriously to themselves than in relation to medical science.   It has
entirely prevented them from becoming acquainted with
the anatomy of the human body, or the nature and relation to each other of its various organisms.   Their
medical knowledge is entirely empirical, their knowledge
of surgery is *nil*.   The result has been the prevalence of
untold suffering in many forms.   Christian physicians
and surgeons have, in consequence, found among the
crowded populations of the Chinese cities a vast and
needy field for the exercise of their skill, and medical
missions have become one of the most popular and efficient means of reaching the Chinese.   Philanthropy,
manifested on a very large scale and under circum-

stances of peculiar trial by the missionaries and the Christian public of Great Britain and America, has been another powerful influence in removing prejudice and presenting Christianity to the people in a favourable light. The great alluvial plains of North and Central China have been subjected to alternate floods and droughts on a scale of magnitude almost impossible to realize. " China's sorrow", the Yellow River, has been responsible for the most serious of these calamities. In the famine which prevailed in Shantung and Shansi in 1876–77, and which was continued farther north in the two following years, it has been estimated that several millions (some have said thirty millions) perished. The missionaries who were at work in the districts most seriously affected at once devoted themselves with splendid self-sacrifice to the hard work of administering the relief which came in response to their appeals. Many thousands owed their lives to this help, and the benevolence of Christianity produced a profound effect for good upon multitudes, and extorted the gratitude even of the emperor.

Notwithstanding these helpful influences the hostility to Christianity in China has been ceaseless and violent. The *literati*, conservative to the backbone and filled with the proud sense of the absolute superiority of everything Chinese to everything foreign, probably also dreading more than they cared to admit the introduction of new ideas which would disturb the old order and imperil their own supremacy, have resented all innovation, and have not scrupled to resort to the most violent means for driving out the "foreign superstition ". The history of the Church Missionary Society's Mission at Foochow is an illustration of the pertinacity and ruthlessness of this hostility. It was eleven years before a single convert was won in that mission. No sooner had the first converts been baptized than a riot occurred, in which the whole of the mission premises were utterly destroyed. Since then the mission has progressed so remarkably that its work extends over seventeen counties, and fully 11,000 converts are now to be numbered in the Christian Church created by its agency. Yet only so recently as 1895 the civilized world was horrified by the story of the Kucheng massacre, when, without any apparent warning, an anti-foreign outbreak took place at a prosperous mission station, and eleven members of the missionary circle were cruelly murdered. There are few missionaries of any long experience and prominence in China connected with any of the great societies who have not at some time been stoned, and been in peril of their lives from the violence of the mob. Not a year has passed in which there has not been persecution of native Christians in some part of China, often resulting in loss of life. The Tientsin massacre of 1870, which was directed chiefly against the Roman Catholic Mission, became notorious only on account of the number of the victims, the ruthless cruelty attending the murder of the unfortunate missionaries, and the active measures taken by France to procure punishment or compensation. In 1891-92-93 the whole of Central China was flooded with anti-foreign literature emanating from persons in high position in Changsha, the capital of the province of Hunan, which has been the centre of Chinese conservatism. In these papers, many of which were coarsely but effectively illustrated, the most blasphemous and filthy calumnies were circulated against Christianity and the Christians, and the minds of the people were excited to violent hostility against them.

In spite of this determined opposition the missionary enthusiasm of the Church of Christ has not faltered. Year by year the number of missionaries has increased and the outposts of Christianity have been extended, until every one of the eighteen provinces has been occupied.   There are now upwards of 1384 men and women, including the wives of missionaries, as the representatives of British missions in China, the total number of Protestant missionaries from Great Britain, Europe, and America being 2442.   The number of known converts when China was opened in 1842 was *six*; it is now nearly, if not quite, 90,000.

The story of the early Roman Catholic missions in JAPAN is a profoundly interesting and suggestive one. They were part of the heroic age of the Jesuit Order, and were commenced by Xavier in 1549.   Not only was their numerical success very remarkable, but much of the work they did, by means of the school, the printing-press, and varied literature, was of a very broad and substantial kind.   Unfortunately the progress of Christianity was by those early missionaries associated with the attempt to gain and to exercise political influence, and the hostility of the rulers was speedily aroused.   In 1587 the first edict for the expulsion of missionaries was passed.   In the long persecution that followed, tens of thousands of converts were put to death, and great multitudes suffered cruel punishment and torture.   Under the influence of this spirit of violent antagonism to Christianity, Japan gradually isolated itself from the rest of the world.   Foreign trade came to an end save under the most restricted and humiliating conditions. All native sea-going craft were destroyed.   Japanese who under any circumstances left the country were put to death if they ventured to return.   " The boards which were erected in the seventeenth century at cross-roads and bridges with the proclamation, ' The evil sect called Christians is strictly forbidden; informers will be rewarded ', were not removed until 1869."

The history of modern missions in Japan dates from 1859, when, as the result of the American treaty obtained by Townsend Harris, certain ports were opened to foreigners for trade and residence under severe restrictions. The Roman Catholic Church at once re-entered the country and began to gather up the scattered fragments of its former mission. The American Protestant missions also at once commenced work, and for ten years they were alone in the field. Those early missionaries were the objects of intense suspicion and closest espionage. "They were not only closely confined to the treaty ports, but even there or on their short walks through the 7 *ri* limits, were in danger of life."

In 1868 a great revolution commenced in Japan, which ended, in 1872, by the destruction of feudalism and the complete triumph of the Mikado's government. This was the real beginning of the modern history of Japan. In 1873 the publication of the antichristian laws was discontinued, and they gradually fell into desuetude. In 1889, when a constitutional form of government was granted by the emperor, these laws were formally repealed, and provision was made in the constitution for assuring religious liberty throughout the empire.

British missionary effort in Japan is represented almost entirely by the Church Missionary Society and the Society for the Propagation of the Gospel, and associations connected with one or other of these societies. In 1868 the Church Missionary Society received a special donation for the purpose of establishing a mission in Japan, and sent out its first missionary, the Rev. George Ensor. Four years after (1872), two anonymous donors enabled the Society for the Propagation of the Gospel to follow. The Revs. W. B. Wright and A. C. Shaw were set apart, in July, 1873, as the first missionaries of the Society for the Propagation of the Gospel to Japan, their farewell service being one of the last public appearances of Bishop Wilberforce. In 1883 the bishopric of Japan was established, and in 1887 a Japanese Episcopal Church was formed. "The synod through which this was done, in February, 1887, was a freely-elected body, in which the Europeans and Americans were greatly outnumbered by Japanese, the majority of whom were men of education." "At the same time a Native Missionary Society, directly responsible to the whole Church, was set on foot, and in 1888 it commenced operations by occupying two stations in Tokio and one each at Osaka and Kumamoto." Its latest movement has been the commencement of a mission in Formosa. Largely as the result of the earnest labours of the late Bishop Bickersteth, the "Japan Church" has greatly developed, the Episcopal Mission from the United States co-operating heartily with the Anglican Mission in promoting its interests. The bishopric of Japan has now been divided into seven distinct sees, of which two belong to the American Church.

The Society for the Propagation of the Gospel now carries on its work in Tokio, Kobe, Yokohama, and Fukushima, and has a staff of twelve clergy, of whom five are Japanese. The Church Missionary Society, with its usual energy and courage, occupies twenty stations, and has a staff of upwards of thirty European male missionaries, with a large number of native helpers. The staff of lady workers is also large, and by means of a Divinity School educated Japanese are being prepared for the work of the ministry among their own countrymen.

In 1873 the Methodist Church of Canada began a mission in Japan. The first efforts were confined to Tokio, but they have extended their labours to other places, and now have work in five principal centres.

The United Presbyterian Church of Scotland also commenced work in Tokio in 1874, and maintains two European missionaries who work in close association with the mission established by the American Presbyterian Churches, which are all happily blended in one strong organization as the Presbyterian Union Church.

The "hermit" nation, KOREA, situated between China and Japan, has been quite inaccessible to the world until comparatively recent years. It has not, however, been left entirely without knowledge of Christianity even before its doors began to be opened to the entrance of the missionary. The Rev. John Ross of Moukden, in Manchuria, met some Korean youths nearly thirty years ago, and acquired such a knowledge of their language that he was able to translate the whole of the New Testament into Korean. He sent the book into the country, with large numbers of Chinese Bibles. The result was that when the first missionaries entered the country, they found in Northern Korea considerable communities who were acquainted with Christianity, professed Protestantism, and were waiting for someone to come and teach them.

Mission work was commenced in 1884, and has been mainly carried on by American missionary societies. The Presbyterian Church in Australia maintains a band of missionaries in Korea, working in close association with the American Presbyterian Board. The Society for the Propagation of the Gospel has a chaplain at Chemulpo, but his work is as yet mainly to provide for the spiritual needs of the European community.

While the great heathen countries of Eastern and Southern Asia have thus called forth a very large amount of Christian enthusiasm, and have made very heavy and growing demands upon the purses and the personal consecration of British Christians, Western Asia has not been neglected. The Turkish Empire has been a peculiarly trying field for Christian effort on account of the difficulty, not to say the peril to life as well as property, which has always attended the profession of Christianity by Mohammedans, and the cruelly harsh treatment of all the members of the ancient Christian churches who live under Turkish rule. Persia has, until quite recently, been closed to Christian workers, and the influence of Mohammedanism through-out the whole of Arabia has been an effectual hindrance to missionary labour on any extended scale. These difficulties, however, have not been effectual to prevent effort, and faith has been rewarded by gradual diminu-tion in the obstacles.

Syria and Palestine have naturally attracted the sympathetic attention of many, and various attempts have been made to carry on mission work. The Church Missionary Society, on the urgent appeal of Bishop Gobat, commenced a mission in Palestine in 1851, and has been greatly encouraged by the result. Jerusalem, Nazareth, Joppa, Nablous, Gaza, and several other places are the centres of the work. Three hospitals, and upwards of forty schools, with 2500 scholars, are maintained by the mission, and a considerable staff of English ladies are associated with the missionaries as workers among the women.

The Free Church of Scotland commenced a medical mission in the Lebanon in 1872. The Friends' Syrian Mission, now amalgamated with the Friends' Foreign Mission Association, occupied Brumana in the Lebanon in 1874. They also have a medical mission and a number of schools, and their lady workers find a welcome among the women of many villages.

The British Syrian School Society was formed by Mrs. Bowen Thompson in 1860. There are also several personal missions.

In 1888 the Hon. and Mrs. Ion Keith-Falconer visited Southern Arabia, and tried to find a suitable locality for commencing a mission. Finally they decided on establishing themselves on British territory in the neighbourhood of Aden. In the following year they returned with a medical missionary, and began work at Shaikh Othman. Within a few months Mr. Keith-

Falconer died, but the mission was endowed by his family in memory of him, and is worked in connection with the Free Church of Scotland. The medical services of the missionary are appreciated by an ever-increasing number of Arabs, and thus by degrees the prejudice which has been so general and so bitterly opposed to Christianity has gradually yielded.

The work which the Church Missionary Society is now carrying on in Persia was commenced privately by the Rev. R. Bruce in 1869 during a visit to Ispahan. Finding that many of those he met were not unwilling to discuss the claims of Christianity in a friendly way, he decided to remain there for their instruction. In 1875 his mission was adopted by the Church Missionary Society, and in 1882 it was extended to Baghdad. Kirman and Yerd are also stations of the mission. It is not easy to estimate the real results of this work as yet, on account of the risks involved in a profession of Christianity. Every report contains illustrations of the oppression and persecution of the Christians at the instigation of the Mohammedan mullahs. There are, however, nearly 600 baptized converts, and through the influence of the medical mission, and the circulation of the Scriptures and Christian literature, large numbers are being informed and favourably affected towards Christianity.

Chapter III.

Growth during the past Sixty Years.—The Two Atlantic Continents, and the Islands of the Pacific.

Nowhere have the faith, the consecration, the suffering, and the heroism of the Christian Church been more signally and generally manifested than in Africa. At the commencement of the Queen's reign the great interior of the dark continent was practically unknown to the world. The slave-traders had extended their raids far inland both on the east and the west for more than a century. Portuguese or half-caste Portuguese traders penetrated into the interior from both coasts more than two centuries ago. But the knowledge thus gained was kept from the world so completely that so lately as 1851 the President of the Royal Geographical Society was able to say, "All beyond the coast of Central South Africa is still a blank on our maps". The opening up of Africa was due in the first instance to the labours of two missionaries, and ever since missionaries have been among the foremost to press on into the unknown, and the opening up of every new region has constituted a new call to consecration and service. In 1843 Ludwig Krapf, a missionary of the Church Missionary Society, was expelled from Abyssinia and went down the east coast to Zanzibar, and thence to Mombasa, where he settled at the beginning of 1844. After a few months he was joined by a colleague, John Rebmann, and soon they began to visit the tribes in the interior. In 1848 Rebmann first sighted Kilima Njaro. Next Krapf saw from afar Mount Kenia, and the location of the traditional "Mountains of the Moon" was set at rest. In the course of this journey Krapf heard from Arabs and natives of a vast inland sea somewhere in the interior. These discoveries and reports raised such interest that the Royal Geographical Society in 1857 sent out an expedition under Burton and Speke, who, in the following year, reached Lake Tanganyika and the southern shore of the Victoria Nyanza. In 1862 Speke, with Grant, reached Uganda, and discovered the Somerset Nile flowing out of it to the north.

Meanwhile in South Africa another missionary traveller was quietly at work, who was destined to carve

his name very deeply and indelibly on the map of
Central Africa, and whose labours have had a unique
influence on missionary development and philanthropic
effort.   David Livingstone, the weaver lad from Blantyre, who had fought his way to knowledge with the
indomitable perseverance which was one of his most
marked characteristics, learning Latin by keeping his
book on the loom as he worked, and obtaining a
university course in Glasgow in the intervals of toil,
was accepted by the London Missionary Society for
service in China, but in consequence of the outbreak of
war with that country his destination was changed
to South Africa much against his inclination.   In 1841
he landed in Cape Town and proceeded to Bechuanaland, where he found an opening among the Bakwena
under Sechele.   In 1849, in company with an English
gentleman named Oswell, he discovered Lake Ngami.
Two years later he first sighted the Zambesi, and in
1853 he commenced that adventurous journey from
Linyanti to Loanda on the west coast, which first
brought him prominently into notice.   His return journey from Loanda to Quillimane was the first known
feat of the kind, and has all the merit of a first performance.   His success as a traveller was doubly note-
worthy because, unlike the majority of other modern
travellers and explorers in Central Africa, he was very
poorly equipped, and also because, notwithstanding all
the risks to which he was exposed, especially when he
came within the region of the slave-trader, he was able to
say he had never fired a shot in attack or in self-defence.
Livingstone's soul was stirred within him by what he saw
on his first journey of the horrors of the African slave
traffic, and he determined to devote the rest of his life
to the opening up of Africa in the interests of freedom,
civilization, and Christianity.   When, on the morning
of May 4, 1873, he was found by his faithful followers

dead in his hut at Ilala, near far-off Lake Bangweolo, it was in the attitude of prayer, a touching commentary on his own words that "the end of the geographical feat is the beginning of the enterprise". Other men have crossed Africa since his day from west to east, and from east to west. Its vast inland seas, its mighty rivers, its dense populations, have all been revealed to the world. There is scarcely a district of any size which does not bear upon it the impress of the foot of the eager explorer, and "spheres of influence" have been jealously claimed and competed for by great European nations in lands which, less than half a century ago, were believed to be barren wastes, utterly valueless. Yet it is no exaggeration to say that no other explorer has quite taken the same place as Livingstone in the popular imagination, or has had so marked an influence in the development of Africa. The Universities Mission in East Africa was commenced at his appeal. The Livingstonia Mission of the Presbyterian Churches on Lake Nyassa was a monument to him. The Central Africa Mission of the London Missionary Society was established on Lake Tanganyika because there he had last been seen by white men. Sir H. M. Stanley's journey to Tanganyika in search of Livingstone, in the interests of a great newspaper, and the impression which intercourse with Livingstone made upon him, changed his career from a newspaper correspondent to a great explorer. It was Stanley's appeal from Uganda that led to the commencement of the Church Missionary Society Mission there, and it was Stanley's discovery of the Upper Congo that opened the way for the establishment of the Congo Mission of the Baptist Missionary Society and the Congo Balolo Mission of Dr. Grattan Guinness. Thus the influence, direct or indirect, of one humble missionary, turned by God's providence at the beginning of his career out of the path in which he desired to walk, and sent to Africa against his wishes, has been the means of bringing the gospel to the whole of Central Africa.

Mission effort in Africa before the commencement of the Queen's reign was very restricted in area and very limited in amount. The Mohammedan States in North Africa were closed against missionaries. The Church Missionary Society had, it is true, commenced a mission in Egypt in 1825 in which Gobat, afterwards Bishop of Jerusalem, was one of the first workers. Gobat in 1830 succeeded in gaining an entrance to Abyssinia, and an interesting mission was commenced there. But both these efforts were directed rather to the enlightenment and revival of the ancient Coptic and Abyssinian Churches than to the conversion of the heathen or Mohammedans. Down the whole east coast there was not in 1837 a single mission station or missionary except in the extreme south, in the part of Kaffirland bordering on Cape Colony. On the west coast there was the same absolute dearth from Namaqualand in the south to Sierra Leone, a distance of fully 4000 miles. At Sierra Leone the Church Missionary Society had been at work since 1804, some of their first missionaries having been sent out to the Rio Pongas in that year. The Wesleyans also had occupied Sierra Leone since 1811, and in 1831 had begun another mission still farther up the coast on the River Gambia. Both these missions were suffering severely from the climate and were in a very weak state.

The emancipation of the West Indian slaves was, as has already been pointed out, the means of quickening interest in the evangelization of Africa, and the progress of discovery stimulated effort in new directions. The result has been a remarkable development of missionary enterprise, with a story of romantic interest. Great Britain has not been by any means alone in the attempt to evangelize Africa. The fascination of its great needs has drawn to it the attention of the Christians of America, France, Holland, Germany, Switzerland, Norway, Sweden, and Finland. From all sides earnest workers are pushing steadily on towards the centre.

In South Africa, notwithstanding many difficulties, partly due to the prevalence of strong racial feeling of contempt for the coloured races, and partly to the frequent fierce wars in which the natives vainly strove to prevent the constant encroachment of the white man, mission work has been prosecuted with vigour and with marked success. The London Missionary Society was for many years conspicuous through the labours of the Rev. Dr. Philip of Cape Town, and others, for its vindication of the rights of natives against the oppressions of the colonists. It maintained a strong mission in many of the principal towns of the Cape Colony and in settlements specially provided by the Government as refuges for the natives. In 1856 the directors decided that the time had arrived when the churches within the Cape Colony should begin to undertake the burden of self-support. Within the next ten years the movement was completed, and almost without exception the colonial stations became independent churches, receiving occasional help in times of emergency, but henceforth managing their own affairs. At the same time, in consequence of the strength of the Wesleyan and Presbyterian missions in Kaffirland, the society began to restrict its efforts in that direction and to devote itself more exclusively to extension northward. The names of Robert Moffat, David Livingstone, and John Mackenzie are only the most prominent among a noble band of missionaries. Bechuanaland and Matabeleland have in recent years gradually absorbed all its efforts in South Africa.

The work of the Wesleyans has spread in many directions. Within the two British colonies it is not easy to distinguish their mission to the natives from their provision for the spiritual needs of the white population. Every colonial town of any size has a Wesleyan church. They have maintained a strong and successful mission among the Kaffirs. They have a mission among the Zulus. Moving northward on a line parallel to the work of the London Missionary Society, but farther east, they have a mission among the Barolongs at Thaba N'chu in the Free State, and also among the branch of the same tribe resident near Mafeking in Bechuanaland. They are actively engaged in work among the natives in the Transvaal. They have reached Mashonaland, and have also now begun work in Western Rhodesia.

The Presbyterian societies have not been so expansive in their efforts, but their missions in Kaffirland are exceptionally strong and well developed, and they have been honoured with a remarkable succession of able missionaries. The work in Kaffraria was originally commenced in 1824, and was for a number of years carried on by the "Glasgow Missionary Society". In 1837 that society was broken in two on the question of Church Establishments; the larger number of missionaries remained in connection with that section which was known as the "Glasgow Society adhering to the principles of the Church of Scotland". The rest joined the Glasgow African Missionary Society. The latter in 1847 was merged in the United Presbyterian Church; while at the disruption of the Church of Scotland in 1843 the whole of the missionaries belonging to the older section followed the same course as their brethren in India, and joined the Free Church. The happy result has been two strong missions working side by side in thorough good fellowship. The work of the Free Church of Scotland has been conspicuously strong from an educational point of view. Both missions have vigorous self-supporting native churches with local Presbyterian government. The visit of Dr. Duff of Calcutta to South Africa led to the establishment in 1867 by the Free Church of Scotland of a mission in Natal. In 1874 the Gordon Memorial Mission in Natal in connection with the same Church was founded and endowed by the Dowager Countess of Aberdeen and her family in memory of the Hon. J. H. Gordon, who had wished to be a missionary in South Africa.

Episcopal missions in South Africa owe their origin to the remarkable personal influence of Bishop Gray, the first Bishop of Cape Town, consecrated in 1847. He was a thorough Churchman, but also a man of broad human sympathies and great organizing power. Before his death in 1872 he had the satisfaction of seeing his province divided into seven dioceses, and a remarkable circle of missionary bishops at work. The earliest of these was Bishop Armstrong, who in 1854 took the eastern province and Kaffraria, and who determined to begin work in Kaffirland proper. Armstrong was followed after two years by Bishop Cotterill. He in turn was succeeded in 1871 by Bishop Merriman as Bishop of Grahamstown, and a separate bishopric of Kaffraria was commenced, the first occupant of the see being Bishop Callaway. Both Merriman and Callaway were very remarkable men. Dr. Callaway abandoned a lucrative medical practice in London for the work of an evangelist, and for nearly twenty years " without a break had so laboured among the people as to have acquired an intimate knowledge of their modes of thought, their folk-lore, and their language. His manifold gifts as physician, farmer, printer, as well as priest, had been freely exercised for their benefit."

The first Bishop of Natal was Dr. Colenso, who was appointed in 1855. His opinions on questions of the Higher Criticism, and his relations to the ecclesiastical

community of which he was the head, are outside the
scope of the present work, but his memory will long be
cherished by the natives of Natal as that of their self-
sacrificing and faithful friend and constant champion.
No man has more thoroughly mastered the language
and the history of the Kaffirs, or has been more
thoroughly trusted and respected by them. The advance of the Episcopal Church in South Africa is seen
in the fact that bishoprics have been established in
Zululand, Bloemfontein, Pretoria, Mashonaland, and
Lebombo. None of these are purely missionary sees,
but all of them owe their origin to the missionary
activity of the Church, and are largely concerned with
missionary work among the natives.

In 1870 the Primitive Methodist Society commenced
a mission in the Cape Colony, which, though small,
has been vigorously and successfully maintained. The
only other British missionary organization at work in
South Africa is the South African General Mission.
It was started originally as a railway mission, to meet
the spiritual needs of the scattered employees on the
various lines of railway. In 1889 it was reorganized
as a general evangelistic mission among the English-
speaking population in the colonial towns. Since then
it has also been directly engaged in work among the
natives.

All the missions in South Africa, especially those
labouring on the south-east coast, have passed through
successive storms of very severe trial in connection with
the Kaffir and Zulu wars. Notwithstanding their difficulties every mission has been greatly prospered. They
all have associated with them native clergy and
ministers of undoubted ability and high character. The
Bantu races are much less impulsive, much slower to
move, than the negroes. They are thrifty and acquisi-
tive, tenacious, intelligent, ambitious. There is already

as the result of missionary labour a nucleus of men of some education and of undoubted capacity who are beginning to look out on all the great questions of political life and government with great shrewdness and a growing sense of their own strength. Among the many problems of South Africa there is none which will require wiser handling or a more dispassionate and steadfast grasp of great Christian principles than that of the position which educated and christianized natives are to take in the great mixed community which is filling the land.

Missionary effort on the west coast of Africa has also extended enormously during the last forty years, in spite of difficulties which in some districts have made the history of the work one long tragedy. West Africa has well been called the "White Man's Grave". Missionary records have confirmed this title with sad emphasis. In the mission of the Church Missionary Society in Sierra Leone, deaths came so rapidly and in such numbers, that again and again in the earlier history of the mission it seemed as if the work must be given up. The first three bishops died within seven years. The Wesleyans, who were next in the field, had the same experience. "From one point of view, the whole history of the Sierra Leone Mission seems but a mournful sacrifice of young lives. In the course of fifty years, sixty-three missionaries had lost their lives through the climate of West Africa, or had died at sea when proceeding to or from their appointments." The United Presbyterian Mission was commenced by men seasoned by residence in the climate of Jamaica, yet they also have lost fully thirty men and women from the effects of climate, while others have been forced to retire. The Baptists on the Cameroons, and more recently and more painfully on the Congo, have had the same sad experience. The conditions of the work have also been of an exceptionally trying kind in consequence of the appalling superstition and the revolting and atrocious cruelty of the negro tribes. Yet there is not a mission on the west coast which has not amply justified its existence and proved a potent force for great social and spiritual change.

The Church Missionary Society received a warm commendation in 1842 from a Parliamentary Committee of Enquiry at Sierra Leone, who testified that crime had greatly decreased and the general standard of morality and conduct had been greatly raised as the result of mission work. That mission in Sierra Leone has steadily advanced educationally and religiously. In 1862 the Episcopal Church of Sierra Leone was organized, "most of the parishes had native pastors, supported by native funds through a Church Council".

The people of Sierra Leone were liberated slaves, and they were born traders. Some of the converts bought a vessel and went on a trading expedition along the Slave Coast as far as Badagry. This resulted in opening up communication with Abeokuta, and ultimately in 1846 the commencement by the Church Missionary Society of a mission in the Yoruba country was decided on. That mission in its sorrows and its successes has evoked a very wide-spread interest and sympathy, and, notwithstanding determined efforts of the slave-trader and the heathen, has prospered greatly. This Yoruba country was the birthplace of Samuel Crowther, the story of whose life is a chapter in the veritable romance of missions, as well as a signal illustration of the possibilities which exist even in the most degraded races. Crowther was carried into slavery as a child by a band of native marauders, was sold for a horse, and returned to the seller as a bad bargain, sold again more than once for rum and tobacco, and finally sold to a Portuguese to be exported. The day after the vessel in which he was carried off started, she was captured by a British cruiser and taken into Sierra Leone, where the youth found himself free, and was handed over to the care of the mission. He showed remarkable aptitude in acquiring knowledge, and from the first began also to learn the spiritual lessons of the gospel. From school in Sierra Leone he was taken to England and placed at a school in London for a few months. Returning to Sierra Leone he became the first student in the Fourah Bay College in 1827. In 1840 Sir T. Fowell Buxton and others formed an association for the civilization of Africa, and persuaded H.M. Government to send out an expedition for the exploration of the lower waters of the River Niger. A missionary of the Church Missionary Society, Mr. Schön, and young Crowther, who was then a Scripture-reader, accompanied that ill-fated expedition. His character came out so markedly that he was invited to England by the society, received further training, and in 1843 was ordained to the ministry. In 1846 he was commissioned by the society to go with Mr. Townsend to Abeokuta to commence the Yoruba Mission, and one of the first six converts who were baptized was his own mother, from whom he had been torn by the slave raiders twenty-seven years before, and whom he met accidentally in the road. For eleven years he laboured in the Yoruba Mission, and then in 1857 went to the Niger, established himself at Onitsha, and thus opened the third great mission of the Church Missionary Society on the west coast of Africa. He was consecrated Bishop of the Niger in 1862, and laboured in the development of the work of his diocese until his death in 1891. In the delta of the Niger there is now an important, growing, self-supporting native Church, while from the upper Niger an effort is being made to reach the Soudan.

The missions of the Wesleyan Missionary Society

occupy the same region as that in which the work of
the Church Missionary Society is chiefly situated, viz.
Sierra Leone and the Gambia River; Lagos, Abeokuta,
and other places in the Yoruba country; and the Gold
Coast. This probably arises from the fact that both
missions at the outset sought to make special provision
for the freed slaves and other inhabitants of the British
settlement of Sierra Leone, and that they have spread
out from thence. Sickness and sorrow are the melan-
choly record of the early years of the mission. The
great mortality among European workers has, however,
resulted in special efforts to train a native ministry.
The work is now mainly in the hands of natives. The
chief pastorates, the upper as well as the elementary
schools, and also the Training Institution for Ministers,
are now under the care of those who, half a century ago,
were themselves heathen. The small staff of English
missionaries exercise the functions of an episcopate as
"superintendents" of districts, or are leaders in the
pioneer mission work in the regions beyond. The
churches in Free Town, St. Mary's Island, Lagos, and
other chief centres of life are strong and self-supporting,
and are taking an active part in conveying the gospel
to the heathen tribes of the interior.

As has already been noted, the emancipation of the
slaves in the West Indies led to a remarkable development of missionary zeal on the part of the Christian
negroes for their kinsfolk still in Africa. The earliest
result of this movement was the mission of the Baptist
Missionary Society in the Cameroons. The Rev. J.
Clarke of Jamaica and Dr. Prince went out to the west
coast on a tour of inspection. They decided to begin
work at Clarence in the island of Fernando Po, and a
church of five members was formed there in 1842. Then
they visited Jamaica and England, and roused great
enthusiasm among the Baptist congregations on behalf

of the new mission. Especially they caught the ear and the heart of Alfred Saker, a man of twenty-eight, a wheelwright, of vigorous mind and keen intelligence, and occupying a good position in the engineering department of H.M. Dockyard at Devonport. He was an earnest Christian and a zealous worker. He and his wife offered themselves for the service, were accepted, and went out in 1843. Henceforth he became the leading spirit in the mission. After various mechanical labours at Clarence, in 1845 he went across to the mainland accompanied by an earnest Jamaican negro, Horton Johnson. They found a place for work at King A'Kwa's town, twenty miles from the coast, among the Dualles, a notoriously degraded and drunken tribe. He learned the language, set up a printing-press, practised medicine, lived for the people, and at last after four years gained his first convert. Then he had to go home, completely broken down in health, leaving the mission in the care of Mr. Newbiggin, who died almost immediately. There had been so many deaths before this, that there were serious thoughts of giving up the mission, but Saker protested and went back to Africa in 1851. He found that during his absence the work had made true progress. A time of rich spiritual blessing followed. "Under Saker's guidance the arts of civilization went hand in hand with religion; he dug a clay pit and made bricks, he wrought as a carpenter, and a worker in metals, and planted a kitchen garden. The printing-press was constantly busy, . . . class-books were prepared, and portions of the Scriptures were translated." Meanwhile the Church prospered at Clarence, and the work at Bimbin progressed.

Then the Spaniards upset the mission. They had annexed the island of Fernando Po in 1845, but promised religious liberty to the Protestants. In 1848 an edict was issued forbidding, under severe penalties, all religious

worship save that of the Roman Catholic Church.   The
Baptist converts had to decide to give up their faith or
to migrate.   They chose the latter course.   A place was
found some distance up the coast on which a new settlement was formed, which was named Victoria.   This
prospered, and the mission in other places was pressed
forward.   In 1876 Saker was forced to retire, quite
worn out with his manifold labours, and he died in 1880.
Meanwhile George Grenfell had joined the mission in
1874, and was gaining an experience which was to prove
invaluable in after-days.   In 1884 the Germans annexed
the Cameroons, and difficulties arose between the
missionaries and the German authorities, which finally
led in 1887 to the transfer of the mission to the Basel
Missionary Society.

Thomas Comber and George Grenfell while at work
in the Cameroons made frequent attempts at exploration
and extension into the interior.   In 1877 these efforts
were turned in a special direction by an offer of £1000
by Mr. Robert Arthington towards the establishment of
a mission in the Congo country.   The visit of Comber
and Grenfell to San Salvador was the beginning of one
of the most remarkable and heroic missionary ventures
of modern times.   The great basin of the Congo with
all its tributaries represents a population of probably
40,000,000, the vast majority of whom are barbarians
enslaved by the grossest superstitions, and practising
horrible cruelties.   The influence of the white man has
been to deepen the degradation and increase the cruelty.
H. M. Stanley, in his great journey down the Congo,
testified that in the far interior he could pay his way
and purchase food with ordinary barter goods of calico,
beads, &c.   When he approached the zone of the white
man's influence gunpowder and firearms became increasingly the only acceptable barter.   Ultimately he
reached a region where even guns were at a discount,

and the one thing which was acceptable was rum. When he arrived at this point he was within reach of the traders, and he had to send forward and obtain supplies of the hateful currency before he could complete his journey to the coast. The Baptists were the pioneers of Christian work in this great region, and their success has been in the measure of their courage, their suffering, and their consecration. The story is still recent, and the chief actors have not all of them left the stage, consequently it is too early for dispassionate history. The mission has been pushed steadily up the river, until its most advanced posts are upwards of 1000 miles from the coast. Its first converts were baptized at San Salvador in 1886, now they number 267, while 1111 children are in their schools.

The Congo Balolo Mission—now known as the "Regions Beyond Missionary Union"—was commenced in 1889, and is pushing on its work vigorously along the southern affluents of the great river. Several other societies, American and Continental, are now sharing in the great enterprise of evangelizing this vast region.

The Old Calabar Mission of the United Presbyterian Church was another outcome of the awakening among the West Indian Negroes as the result of emancipation. For two years the possibility of such an effort was thought of and discussed among the Presbyterian Mission Churches in Jamaica. Then in 1841 the publication of Sir T. Fowell Buxton's book on *The Slave Trade and its Remedy* brought the thoughts to fruition. At a meeting of the Jamaica Presbytery of the United Presbyterian Church each of the eight members in turn pledged himself to go to Africa if called to do so. The Rev. Hope M. Waddell became the first missionary, and landed on April 10, 1846, at Duke Town, Old Calabar, accompanied by a printer, a carpenter, and a teacher.

The superstition and degradation of the people amongst whom they sought to settle was appalling, though they carried on a considerable trade and had abundant wealth.   They murdered all twins.   They were utterly reckless of human life: hecatombs of victims were slaughtered when a great chief died, and slaves were sacrificed without scruple on the slightest pretext.   Marriage was absolutely unknown among the slaves, and was rare even among the free men. When the chief Eyamba died, "chiefs offered up their slaves.   Husbands returned from the fields and found their wives murdered.   Even boys and girls were not exempted.   .   .   .   A pit was dug, and Eyamba was laid in it in state on two sofas.   His sword-bearer, snuff-box carrier, and umbrella holder were taken to the side of the grave, their heads were knocked off, and they were tumbled into a pit with numerous other attendants.   Eyamba had a hundred wives.   Thirty of these were sent into the next world to accompany their master."[1]

Another evil custom, constantly in use, was the trial by ordeal by drinking the esere bean, especially for charges of witchcraft.   The missionaries, as soon as they gained the ear of the people, attacked all these evil customs, and were successful in getting every one of them given up.   From the first they were active in the work of education and in providing books.   Some portions of the Scriptures in the Efik language were printed within six months after the mission was commenced.

The first three stations were Duke Town, Old Town, and Creek Town—all very near each other at the mouth of the Old Calabar River.   Others were opened in the interior at intervals as opportunity offered.   In every one of the earlier extensions the same difficulties had to be surmounted as in the stations at the coast, but in

[1] *Story of the Mission in Old Calabar*, p. 29.

every case Christian influence has been effectual to abolish old evil practices. The first baptisms took place in 1853, and in 1872 the first native convert was ordained as the first native minister.

The mission was fortunate from the outset in its leaders, men acclimatized by residence in Jamaica, acquainted with the negro character, and strong and wise as well as earnest and enthusiastic. Hope M. Waddell, William Anderson, and Alexander Robb were all strong men, and two of them were permitted to labour for many years. They were splendidly seconded by a band of young men and women. The work has developed in various directions. A medical mission was commenced very early in the mission history. The printing-office has been a great power. Finally, in 1893 an institution was opened for industrial training, as well as to be a high school and a place of training for native ministers.

In addition to these larger missions, work has been commenced on a smaller scale by the United Methodist Free Churches at Sierra Leone in 1859. The Primitive Methodist Church also commenced work on the island of Fernando Po in 1869 as the result of the labour of a godly ship's carpenter whose vessel was detained there several months, and who occupied his enforced leisure by conducting services with the natives whom he could gather round him. These were the remnants of the Baptist Mission broken up by the Spaniards. Mr. Hands appealed to the Primitive Methodist Conference on his return to England, and two missionaries were sent out in 1870 in response to the appeal.

Within the watershed of the Congo, though far removed even from the most advanced posts of all other missions, is the Garenganze Mission, which is practically midway between the eastern and the western coasts. The Garenganze Mission is not connected with any of the great missionary societies. It was founded by a young Scotchman, F. S. Arnot, in 1886. Mr. Arnot went out to South Africa in 1881 with the high and heroic purpose to find some place where men had not yet heard the gospel. He worked his way up country from Natal to Northern Bechuanaland with very small resources, depending upon such opportunities of proceeding from point to point as might be offered him by the kindness of traders or hunters, and strong in faith that he would thus be led by God to his destined sphere of work. From Shoshong, the capital of Khama's country, he proceeded with a party of Khama's hunters towards the Zambesi. Ultimately, after a most adventurous journey of peril and suffering, he reached the country of Garenganze, an elevated and healthy region inhabited by a large and powerful tribe of exceptional intelligence. Here he was well received, and decided to commence his permanent work. After a time he was joined by others, who responded to his appeal for help, and the mission became thoroughly established.

East equatorial Africa was the happy hunting-ground of the slave-trader long after the export of slaves from the west coast had been effectually stopped by the closing of the markets as well as by the vigilance of the cruisers. On the east coast even now, the capture of an occasional Arab dhow carrying slaves proves that the trade is not yet entirely dead, nor will it be as long as there is a demand for African slaves in Arabia. For every slave successfully exported, certainly a score of persons —some would say fully a hundred—perished in the tribal wars in which the slaves were captured; from want, in the regions desolated by war; and from the fatigue and cruelties of the long journey to the coast. Half-castes from the Portuguese colonies at the mouth of the Zambesi, and Arabs who had their head-quarters at Zanzibar and other settlements on the coast, were the active and unscrupulous agents of the traffic, and they did their best to prevent any knowledge of their doings from reaching the outer world. Missionary effort in Eastern Africa seemed to be impossible in the year when the Queen ascended the throne. Among the many beneficent movements which have marked Her Majesty's reign there is none which has stayed a larger amount of human misery or brought new possibilities of blessing to a wider area than that which has resulted in breaking up the old combination of slave-traders in Zanzibar and has opened up equatorial Africa to Christian and civilizing influences.

The earliest missionary effort on this side of Africa was that of the Church Missionary Society, commenced by Dr. Krapf and Rebmann at Mombasa in 1844. Rebmann toiled on patiently at Rabai on the hills above Mombasa for twenty-nine years, even after he had totally lost his sight, and died at his station without having visited Europe during the whole of that time. Krapf, by publishing to the world the results of the explorations made by his companion and himself, was, as we have already seen, the means of stimulating British enterprise to that series of remarkable exploratory journeys by which the long-hidden secrets of the dark continent were revealed to the world. Krapf did more than this. He was a great linguist who did most valuable work for those who followed him, and he was a missionary enthusiast of very bold and far-reaching ideas and plans, who dreamed of a chain of mission stations across Africa from Mombasa. Notwithstanding Krapf's energy, Mombasa Rabai Mission languished for years, and there was no other attempt to commence work in East Africa until 1861. In that year two new societies entered the field, very different from each other, and working on very different lines, but each destined to do a very important work. Dr. Krapf's account of his journeys had arrested the attention and stirred the hearts of one or two influential leaders of the United Methodist Free Churches, who felt that in his account of the condition of East Africa a call from God came to them to endeavour to supply the need. The result was a determination to commence a mission. Dr. Krapf, who had returned to England in ill-health, assisted in the selection of the missionaries, accompanied them to Africa, and rendered them invaluable assistance. Within a very few months two of the four missionaries gave up the work disheartened, and a third had to return to Europe, a complete wreck from the effects of the climate. Mr. Wakefield was left alone. Krapf helped him to settle at Ribé, sixteen miles north of Mombasa, and then he had also to return to Europe prostrate. In the following year the Rev. Charles New joined the solitary worker. Since then the mission has had a most chequered history. Man after man has joined it only to die or return home invalided after a few months. One missionary with his wife and a number of converts were massacred. New died quite alone in 1875 during a journey in the interior, having during his comparatively short missionary career proved himself a man of exceptional enterprise, industry, and devotion to the great work on account of which he had gone to Africa. Wakefield laboured on until 1887. The mission has steadily aimed at reaching the Gallas of Abyssinia, and is prospering through sacrifice.

On January 1, 1861, Archdeacon Mackenzie of Natal was consecrated missionary Bishop of the Zambesi, and thus was definitely inaugurated another mission. It was the answer of the British universities, Oxford, Cambridge, Dublin, and Durham, to the appeal made by Dr. Livingstone in 1857, and renewed by the Bishop of Cape Town in 1859. The mission was settled under Livingstone's guidance at Magomero, in the

Shiré highlands. Six months after reaching the station the saintly Mackenzie died from exposure and fatigue. Other deaths rapidly followed, and doubts were expressed of the possibility of carrying on the mission in consequence of the unexampled combination of untoward circumstances—war, famine, and pestilence —with which it had to contend. The bishopric was offered to the Rev. W. G. Tozer. The acceptance of this offer resulted in the connection with the mission of his close friend, the Rev. Edward Steere. "As Dr. Steere put it himself in a speech long afterwards, ' It seemed to me an unworthy thing to send one's best friend into the middle of Africa and to stay comfortably at home one's self, so I volunteered to go with him for a year or two and see him settled'." Steere was a man of exceptional gifts; he was trained for the Bar, was an early leader in the Guild of St. Alban, and as a writer had already proved his power of keen discernment and forceful utterance. Above all, he was a man of strong convictions of duty. This offer was the commencement of nineteen years of splendid service. Strong, able, and energetic as Bishop Tozer was, it is no disparagement of him to say that Steere made the Universities Mission what it has since become. It was speedily found advisable to remove the mission to Zanzibar, and for the next ten years the work was carried on almost exclusively in that place. Bishop Tozer resigned his position on account of continued ill-health in 1872, and Steere succeeded him. During the next eight years his power as a leader came out in many directions. The mission press, which was often worked by his own hands, gained a reputation among the public for the accuracy and thoroughness of its work. Christchurch, built on the site of the old slave-market at Zanzibar, not only after his design, but under his constant personal supervision, is a striking monument of his skill as architect and builder. His literary work was remarkable. He prepared and published a Swahili grammar, dictionary, and other books. When he died in August, 1882, he had translated into Swahili the whole New Testament, a large part of the Old Testament, and the Book of Common Prayer. His great and varied learning and his accurate knowledge on every subject, his wise and always willing practical counsel, his unflinching and clear vindication of principles, his great devotion, his power of managing men, and his sound generalship in ordering the development of the mission, gave him extraordinary influence with all who had to do with him.

The mission extended first to the Usambara country, then to the eastern shore of Lake Nyassa, and finally to the whole district of the Rovuma between Lake Nyassa and the sea. In 1863, when Steere settled at Zanzibar, he had one colleague, and five liberated slave boys were his charge. There are now ninety-four European workers, of whom thirty-eight are ladies. Industrial schools and general education are provided for a large number. A native ministry is already at work.

The appalling waste of life and the shocking atrocities of the east African slave-trade could not long be hidden when missionaries and travellers began to move about. The Church Missionary Society, the Universities Mission, and the Anti-Slavery Society were largely instrumental in keeping the subject before the Government and in obtaining the appointment of Sir Bartle Frere in 1871 on a special mission to Zanzibar, which resulted in a treaty for the suppression of the slave-trade. Another result was the resolve on the part of the Church Missionary Society to resuscitate the Mombasa Mission in a new form. An industrial settlement, which was named Freretown, was founded on the mainland, near Mombasa, with two hundred freed Africans from Nasik as the nucleus, and was speedily increased by large parties of slaves captured from dhows by Her Majesty's cruisers. From this base mission work was pushed inland to the Taita country in 1883. Then farther inland to the Chagga country at the foot of Kilima Njaro in 1885. This was removed to Taveta in 1893. The latest. extension is to Jilore, in the Giriama country north of Mombasa.

Until 1874 nothing had been done for the interior beyond the abortive attempt of the Universities Mission to settle on the Zambesi in 1861. The arrival of Livingstone's faithful servants at the coast with the remains of the great explorer, whose heart they had buried in mid Africa, sent a thrill through all sections of the Christian Church in Great Britain. At once the Presbyterians and the London Missionary Society decided on establishing missions in memory of the great missionary traveller. In Scotland the proposal took shape in a twofold form. A little company of Christian merchants determined to establish in the Lake region a trading corporation which should stop the horrors of the slave-trade at its sources by the competition of legitimate commerce. This African Lakes Company was in close accord with a committee representing the Free Church of Scotland, the Reformed Presbyterian Church, and the United Presbyterians, who decided on forming a joint Christian Mission on Lake Nyassa, to be known as Livingstonia. The Established Church of Scotland also decided on establishing a mission somewhere in the same region. Representatives of both missions went out together on the pioneer expedition in 1875. The Church of Scotland established itself at Blantyre, in the Shiré highlands. The early days of the mission were passed in storm. The station was made a refuge for runaway slaves, and the wrath of the slave-dealers threatened to exterminate the missionaries. It was in a country in which law and order had been wrecked by the slave-trade, and the missionaries unwisely took serious judicial and punitive responsibilities upon themselves. All such difficulties were happily overcome long ago, and the mission has become consolidated and strong. Blantyre, with its schools, its large industrial work, its medical mission, and its handsome church, is quite a centre of civilization and Christian influence. The work has extended to Zomba and also to Domasi, sixty miles to the north.

The Livingstonia Mission has also had its troubles, but has steadily pushed on until it has taken possession of the whole of the west coast of Lake Nyassa from Bandawe on the upper Shiré river to Karonga, near the north end of the lake. From this base-line of more than three hundred miles it is steadily reaching out westwards. From the first the industrial and medical sides of work have been very effectively maintained as well as the purely evangelistic and educational. Twenty years ago there was not a book in any of the languages spoken by the people, nor, if there had been a book, would there have been a native capable of reading it. Now there are upwards of 13,000 children in the mission schools, many of whom show a marked aptitude for learning English. The whole region is now British territory, being included within the domain of the British South Africa Company. The slave-trade is abolished, and commerce is steadily increasing. A recent visitor to one of the stations has given a graphic picture of the change which is going on. "With a free hand and adequate means, Dr. Laws and his earnest helpers will, in a few years, by God's help, completely transform the people of the surrounding country into useful, God-fearing, and law-abiding subjects of the British Empire. Many of them have already in a great measure, through the influence of the mission, given up their gross superstitions and evil heathen customs. It is also quite remarkable

to see the change which has come over the country surrounding the mission station in only three or four years.
Good roads, gardens, fields of country produce, and
Tanganyika wheat, fruits and vegetables of other climes,
and live stock, testify by their appearance to the good-
ness of the country. A quarry which supplies good
building material is not the least attractive sight on the
station, and the industries which supply work and teaching to the people are various and interesting."

The Zambesi Industrial Mission is the latest effort for
the evangelization of this region. It was established in
1892. Its aims are twofold—self-support by cultivation,
and Christian work among the natives who are employed
on the plantations. The prospect of self-support is
already encouraging, and a large number of natives are
under Christian influences.

The two Presbyterian missions had the advantage of
the waterway provided by the Zambesi and Lake Nyassa
to reach their spheres of labour. To the London Missionary Society was given a harder task. It was to
establish itself at the point where Livingstone had last
been seen by Europeans, and, making Ujiji its starting-
point, the whole of the coast of Lake Tanganyika was
to be its sphere of labour, as well as the country to the
south and east of the lake. Mr. Robert Arthington, of
Leeds, who about the same time encouraged the Baptist
Missionary Society to commence a mission on the
Congo, offered £5000 towards the cost of putting a
steamer on the waters of Lake Tanganyika. The attempt to carry out this purpose involved a land journey
of upwards of 830 miles from the nearest point on the
coast, through a country without roads or any means
of conveyance. Long stretches were waterless, many
of the tribes were suspicious and hostile, and the destination was the greatest slave-market in eastern Africa.
The anxiety to provide the new mission with everything

that would be needed at a destination so far removed from the world of civilized life led to a result the opposite of what was desired. The extent of its equipment almost crushed the first party of six missionaries. Two retired, and of the four who ultimately reached Ujiji, two, and those the strongest, and the men from whom most was expected, died almost immediately. The two lay members of the mission survived, but though Mr. E. C. Hore succeeded in gaining the personal friendship of the leading Arabs at Ujiji, and did a large amount of most useful exploratory work on the lake, it soon became apparent that Ujiji, ruled by slave-traders, was a hopeless centre for mission work. A later settlement by Mr. Hore on Kavala island, on the western shore of the lake, and an attempt to work among the Uguha, proved equally fruitless on account of the dread inspired by the trading and slaving caravans which passed that way. The next ten years were years of constant disaster and death. Dr. Mullens, the society's distinguished secretary, died on the journey up with the first relief expedition. Dr. Southon, whose adventurous and remarkable career in his earlier life seemed wonderfully to have trained him for service, and who had made a most promising beginning of work, was accidentally shot. Some died of fever, others retired in broken health. A station was opened among the Wanyamwesi at Urambo, 200 miles to the east of the lake, and others were formed at the south end. One of these is at Niamkolo, on the lake shore; the other two are on the highlands to the south of the lake. The steamer, the offer of which had lured the society on to this distant and hazardous enterprise, was got out by the Zambesi route at enormous cost, was successfully put together and launched, and then it was found that the idea of a mission worked by a steamer to the dwellers around the lake shores was impracticable, and she was sold to the

African Lakes Corporation. In 1897 the station at Urambo, being situated in country that had come under German rule, was handed over to the Moravians, and the society now confines its labours to the sparse population of broken tribes at its three stations at the south end of Lake Tanganyika. Excellent industrial and educational work is being done at these stations. The beginnings of a Christian literature appear, and a small number of Christian teachers are already at work; but the results are small as compared with those of the Presbyterian missions on Lake Nyassa.

Very different has been the history of the mission commenced by the Church Missionary Society to the Victoria Nyanza. In 1876 Mr. Stanley appealed in the *Daily Telegraph* for missionaries to teach M'tesa, the king of Uganda, Christianity, and promised them a hearty welcome. The Church Missionary Society resolved to accept the challenge, and its first party of eight pioneers started in the same year. Among these was A. M. Mackay. Two of the party were murdered, others died; Mackay was the only one who reached Uganda. The story of his life for the next fourteen years is practically the story of the mission: others came and had to leave. Bishop Hannington and a party of men were cruelly murdered by the tyrant Mwanga. Bishop Parker died before he reached his destination. Mackay himself at one time was driven out, but returned and held on. A Scot and a Presbyterian, a son of a Free Church minister in Aberdeenshire, trained as an engineer and successful in his calling, Mr. Mackay gave himself with all the unreserved earnestness of his strong nature to the service of Christ. He went out as a lay assistant to attend to the mechanical and industrial branch of the work. He became the mainstay of the mission, so that when Stanley met a number of the Waganda Christians a few months before Mackay's death, they could only tell him that they were Mackay's children, and belonged to Mackay's mission. What this fourteen years in Uganda meant may be learned from Mackay's letters,[1] or from the *Chronicles of Uganda* or the *Two Kings of Uganda*,[2] or from the diaries of Bishop Hannington. It is one of the most heroic stories in modern missionary history. Mackay's labours and those of his faithful colleagues have not been in vain. Storms of fiery trial have swept over the young Church, but it has weathered the storms. Its foundations have been laid in the blood of hundreds of martyrs, and it is now strong in numbers and progressing rapidly in knowledge.

This region is also under British protectorate, and the changes which have been wrought during the past twenty years are almost incredible. "A road all the way from Mombasa to Port Victoria on the Victoria Lake, a distance of 627 miles, constructed by Capt. Sclater, was completed in 1896. A number of excellent bridges have been made, and bullock wagons have been taken the whole journey. . . . The railway also is advancing, if not rapidly yet surely, into the interior."

The North Africa States have been the home of Mohammedanism ever since the seventh century A.D., and have until quite recent years been jealously closed against any effort to propagate Christianity. Algeria was doubly closed, by Mohammedan hostility and by French law. "With the downfall of the French Empire, and the establishment in its place of the French Republic, religious liberty was granted not only in France, but also in Algeria." The door being opened, the suggestion speedily entered the hearts of one or two earnest men in England that an attempt should be made to send the gospel to the Kabyles. Further enquiry led to

---

[1] *Life of A. M. Mackay*, published by Hodder & Stoughton.
[2] Rev. R. P. Ashe, published by Sampson, Low, & Co., London.

the formation in 1880 of a committee for the purpose of sending out missionaries, and in the following year Mr. Edward Glenny took two young missionaries out as the first-fruits of this movement. In 1883 the mission was reorganized, and has since been known as the North Africa Mission. It has had to encounter and to overcome a very large amount of prejudice and hostility, but has gradually extended its operations, and now has workers in Morocco, Algeria, Tunis, Tripoli, and Lower Egypt. "Its methods of working are by itinerant or localized work, to sell or distribute the Scriptures far and wide, and by public preaching, conversations in the houses, streets, shops, and markets in town and country, to make known those fundamental truths of the gospel a knowledge of which is essential to salvation." Valuable medical work is being done at several centres. "No salary being guaranteed by the mission to the missionaries, their trust must be directly in God for the supply of all their needs." There are no fewer than ninety European workers in connection with the mission under these conditions.

Off the eastern coast of Africa are a number of islands which are more closely connected with it geographically than with any other part of the world, though they give abundant evidence that the connection is only geographical propinquity. In every other respect they belong to quite another region. Many of these islands, such as the Seychelles and Comoros, are small and unimportant. This is not the case, however, with Mauritius and Madagascar, and both these islands are the scene of important British missions.

Mauritius has a population of 377,000, of whom 260,000 are natives of various parts of British India. In addition there are a large number of Chinese. Creole French, English, Tamil, Bengali, Hindi, Chinese, are all to be heard in the streets continually, and those who attempt to engage in Christian work are confronted by a babel of tongues which makes work exceedingly difficult. "English hymns, Hindi *bhajans*, French cantiques, Creole addresses, and Hindi prayers are sometimes heard at the same meeting." The London Missionary Society formerly had a mission in Mauritius, but withdrew in favour of the Church Missionary Society, which still carries on the work under the supervision of the bishop.

Madagascar is one of the largest islands in the world, being 975 miles long by about 350 miles wide, and having an estimated population of from 4,000,000 to 5,000,000. The story of Christian missions in the island during the last sixty years has become familiar to many who are not otherwise specially interested in the work of the London Missionary Society. In 1837 the profession of Christianity was forbidden by the heathen Queen Ranovalona, all Christian books were confiscated, and all who had become Christians were required to renounce their faith. On their refusal to do so, a fierce persecution commenced. At this time there were about 200 avowed Christians in the island, with a considerable number of others who had been under Christian instruction. In the first persecution 17 were put to death, hundreds were made slaves, and a large number only escaped death or slavery by fleeing to the forest, where they remained in the closest hiding, and many died of want and disease. The precious copies of the Scriptures in their possession were buried in secret places, and little companies gathered at midnight to sustain each other's faith and courage by prayer and reading the Word of God. Another persecution broke out in 1849, when 18 persons were put to death, more than 100, with their wives and children, were made slaves, and 2000 were fined. Once more, in 1857, 21 persons were stoned, and 66 were loaded with heavy fetters. Not long after, relief came by the death of the queen in August 1861. Her son, who succeeded to the throne, speedily showed that he was not in sympathy with the policy of his mother, and that his views were enlightened and liberal. Had it not been for personal vices, which ruined his life, he would have been a worthy successor of Radama I. The way being opened for the return of the missionaries, the London Missionary Society sent out a party of six in 1862, including a medical man, a printer, and a schoolmaster. It was found that the knowledge of Christianity had spread secretly, and that there were large numbers in all ranks among the Hova people who were prepared to make a Christian profession. In 1863 Queen Ranovalona II. came to the throne, and in 1869 was baptized on her profession of the Christian faith. She at once burnt publicly the idols belonging to her family, and her action set an example which was followed by thousands. The mission in the centre of the island has since then, and up to the time of the French conquest in 1896, occupied the difficult and perilous position of enjoying the sunshine of royal favour. Queen Ranovalona III., who succeeded her aunt in 1883, was an earnest Christian. The whole of the central province was nominally christianized. The Betsileo also, 200 miles to the south of the capital, were gathered in large numbers into the Church, and missions in the outlying and coast tribes spread rapidly through Hova influence. In 1867 the Friends' Foreign Mission Association commenced work in the island, the London Missionary Society transferring entirely to their care one of the districts on the south-west of the capital, in which work had already been commenced. The Mission of the Friends has never been large in the number of workers, but from the first it has been characterized by a soundness and breadth of policy and a thoroughness of work

which have given it a very distinct and honoured position. In 1863 the Church Missionary Society and the
Society for the Propagation of the Gospel, by friendly
agreement with the London Missionary Society, determined to commence missions on the east coast. After
a time the Church Missionary Society retired from the
field for reasons highly honourable to their Christian
principles. In 1871 an Anglican Bishop of Madagascar
was consecrated in connection with the Society for the
Propagation of the Gospel, and that society began a
mission in the capital.

In addition to these British societies a Norwegian
Mission was commenced in 1867, which has developed
a most successful work on an extended scale among the
Betsileo and the Sakalava tribes.

In 1896 the Hova power was overthrown and the
authority and rule of France were established. At first
the change seemed to threaten ruin to the mission of the
London Missionary Society as the strongest representative of British influence in the island. These difficulties
have now been happily overcome, and work is progressing smoothly, though under greatly changed conditions.

The Atlantic coast of NORTH AMERICA was the earliest field in which the missionary energy of the British
Churches was expended. After the Declaration of Independence, the care of the Indians within the territory
of the United States naturally became the home missionary enterprise of the American Churches, though
financial help was continued from Britain for a considerable time. Now the United States, in the fulness of
their strong, young life, are carrying on missionary
enterprises of their own in all parts of the world on a
scale which rivals, if it does not actually surpass, all
British efforts in missions to the heathen.

In like manner the Canadian colonies of Great Britain,
as their populations have increased in numbers and the

Christian Church in their midst has become strong, have increasingly realized their responsibilities towards the scattered remnants of Indian tribes still to be found on native reserves and in the European townships. Unfortunately, the Indian seems to melt away in contact with European and settled life as snow melts at the breath of the south wind. In the older colonies of Lower Canada there are now very few Indians to evangelize. As the tide of European settlement rolls westward, regions which a few years ago were the remote haunts of the Indian and of large game, become occupied by a settled population engaged in agricultural pursuits, and the Indian is no more. The Dominion of Canada, however, now stretches right across the continent to British Columbia, and includes the vast region which, until 1870, was known as the Hudson's Bay Territory. In the greater part of this region the white man as a settler is not yet known. It is too arctic in the conditions of its climate, and too remote from the outer world, to offer any attractions to any except the hunter and trapper, or more recently, to the gold-seeker. The whole of the North-west Territory, *i.e.* the whole of the Mackenzie River district, Athabasca, Saskatchewan, and the region on the west side of the Rocky Mountains, has been left almost entirely to the Indian tribes.

The Society for the Propagation of the Gospel, in the early days of its work among the settlers of Lower Canada and the other maritime colonies, was not unmindful of the Indians, who were then found in various places. When Upper Canada and the regions beyond were opened up, it undertook some direct missionary work. It still has a mission in the Indian reserve of the province of Ontario, and also in the territory of Manitoba.

In this region the Church Missionary Society has for many years had one of its most interesting and en-

couraging fields of labour.   The endurance and the
heroism of the missionary clergy have been amazing,
and the blessing which has followed their work has been
wonderful.   The first missionary arrived in 1822 at a
trading station on the Red River, which was then a
place in the wilderness, a remote post of the Hudson's
Bay Company.   The Red River district is now the
flourishing colonial province of Manitoba, and a large
part of the society's work has developed into the settled
ministrations of the Church in the colony.   One of the
society's churches has become the Cathedral of the
Diocese of Rupert's Land, founded in 1884.   That
diocese has recently been divided, and again subdivided
into eight.   Upwards of 12,000 Indians are now baptized or under regular instruction, and nearly 2000
children are in the schools.

Nor have Canadian Churches been unmindful of the
claims of this very difficult and important field.   The
Missionary Society of the Methodist Church of Canada
has seventeen stations among the Indian tribes of the
North-west and the west coast, with a membership of
upwards of 1700.   The same society is working among
the Chinese and Japanese, who congregate in such
large numbers in the fisheries and the gold-diggings in
British Columbia.

The Presbyterian Church of Canada is engaged in
similar work, having sixteen stations in the North-west
Territory, and others in British Columbia.   It also
maintains missionaries for work among the Chinese
immigrants.

Passing from North to South America, there are a
number of small, isolated missions among the native
population in the Argentine States, whose work it is not
easy to classify or to describe in detail.   Not a few of them
bear evidence of the great personal devotion and self-

sacrifice of the workers, though the results of their labours would not count for much on a statistical form. The two most important mission fields occupied by British societies are British Guiana on the north-east coast of South America and Terra del Fuego at the extreme south. The former of these fields was entered early in the century by several British societies. The London Missionary Society was the earliest of these. The story of its efforts among the negro population in Demerara and Berbice from 1807 to the time of the Emancipation Act is one which, for the credit of the British colonists, it would be pleasant to be able to blot entirely out of history. From the time when liberty was given by law to the slave and to those who sought his spiritual improvement, the history of the mission has been one of quiet, steady advance, ending in 1874 in independency.

The Church Missionary Society had a mission among the Indians of the Essequibo River from 1831 to 1853, and then withdrew. The Society for the Propagation of the Gospel began its work after the Emancipation Act was passed, and has laboured with great success, not only among the negroes, but also among the Indian aborigines and the coolies imported from India and China. The labours of Mr. W. H. Brett, who settled in 1840 on the Pomeroon River, seem to have been truly apostolic among the Indians. Commencing with the Arawaks, the work extended from them to the Waraws, from them to the Caribs, and finally to the Accawoios. In 1851 more than 1000 Indians had been baptized. Tribes which had never met before except in deadly conflict sat together in happy fellowship at the Lord's Table. The Indians from the inland regions were drawn to the mission, and voluntarily sought for instruction. "From the Potaro and other rivers in the country various tribes sent their embassies to enquire and report, until in 1874 the Government became so convinced of the advantages afforded by the establishment of mission stations among the Indians that it provided stipends for missionary curates on the Pomeroon and Essequibo rivers."[1]

After emancipation it became necessary to import labour for the sugar plantations. In 1845 the importation of coolies from India and China was commenced. In the first four years 120,000 had arrived. They came with all their heathen superstitions, and indulged in a freedom in their worship which would have been forbidden in India. Work among them by the clergy of the Society for the Propagation of the Gospel has been very successful, and they now form an important factor in the Christian life of the country. The results gained among the Chinese coolies have been even more remarkable than among the Hindus.

The South American Missionary Society represents one of the most romantic and heroic efforts of British Christians to reach the heathen. Capt. Allen Gardiner, who was the founder of the mission, had long been anxious to devote his life to the proclamation of the gospel among the most degraded heathen he could find. Among the various schemes which resulted from his travels in various parts of the world was a proposal to the Church Missionary Society in 1836 to establish a mission among the Zulus. This project failed, and he turned his attention to the Indians of Terra del Fuego as being the furthest from hope and help. A society was formed in 1844 known as the Patagonian Missionary Society. The first attempt to communicate with the people was a complete failure, but Gardiner with undaunted courage tried again. In September, 1850, he set sail again with several devoted companions, and with the painful consciousness that very little interest

---

[1] Tucker, *English Church in other Lands*, p. 65.

was felt in his effort by the Christian public. Owing to a series of mistakes and mishaps, the vessel which should have followed them with supplies did not arrive until many months after the time appointed, and was too late. One by one the members of the little band had succumbed to the rigours of the climate and the privations they had to endure. Apparently Gardiner himself was the last to die. When the news reached England public sympathy was aroused, and the South American Missionary Society was formed for the three-fold purpose of ministering to the English in South America, preaching the gospel to the Spaniards, and carrying on missionary work among the Fuegians and other Indian tribes. It was comparatively easy to provide for the first and second portions of the scheme, but the work among the Fuegians was of a different character, and was rooted in tragedy before it bore fruit.

The schooner *Allen Gardiner* went out to the Falkland Islands in 1854, and cautious communication with the Fuegians was commenced. This seemed so promising that in 1859 a party of missionaries decided to settle among them at Woolya on Navarin Island. All went well for a few days, and then on Sunday, November 6, while they were at worship, the whole party were massacred. For three years no further communication was held with the people, and then friendly intercourse was resumed. The result was that in 1868 a settlement was successfully made on Navarin Island, and has steadily gone forward. Ooshooia is now a Christian village, with cottages, a church, a school-house, and an orphanage. Wallaston Island has also become a prosperous industrial and Christian settlement, and the mission is exerting an ever-increasing influence for good.

Missions in the SOUTH PACIFIC were already firmly established in nearly all the principal groups of islands in 1837. Wherever this was the case, the work done since then has been not so much an assault upon heathenism as the slow and patient effort to eradicate the rank and rampant weeds which had run riot for generations of a corrupt and superstitious past, and to prepare the way for the growth of the fruits of Christian life. The islanders had in many cases made a stout resistance to the introduction of Christianity, but when that was over there was a wholesale acceptance of the new religion and renunciation of the old. The work of the London Missionary Society in Tahiti and the Society Group, in the Cook Islands and Samoa, and also that of the Wesleyan Mission in Tonga and Fiji, during the past sixty years, has been that of wise and patient leadership in Christian life rather than of active evangelization. In the early part of the period heathenism still prevailed, especially in Fiji; but, speaking generally, the work of the missionaries throughout the period has been instruction. They have had to introduce and to press forward education, to form a native Church and keep before it worthy ideals of Christian life, and finally, to train a native ministry. This work has been done faithfully and with a considerable measure of success, and the Christian communities in those islands furnish many evidences that they are advancing in the toilsome and difficult upward path to the life of sons of God.

Political changes have affected the missions in various ways. In 1844 the French annexed Tahiti and the Society Islands, and the missionaries of the London Missionary Society were compelled in 1852 to retire. In 1888 the French Protectorate was extended to the Leeward Islands, Raiatea, Tahaa, Borabora, and Huahine, and again it became evident that peaceful work was not possible for an English missionary. These islands have since then been under the care of the Paris Evangelical Missionary Society. On the other hand, the annexation of Fiji by Great Britain in 1874 has secured law and order throughout that extensive group, and has given the work of the Wesleyan Missionary Society a greater stability than before.   The Wesleyans, in addition to the development of their very extensive work in Fiji, have also established a mission in the Island of Rotuma.   The London Missionary Society has extended its efforts in various directions.   A mission was commenced in the Loyalty Islands in 1841.   At that time the inhabitants were among the most fierce, degraded, and inveterate cannibals in the Pacific.   When the French annexed the islands in 1864 they were already changed into peaceful, civilized communities of professing Christians.   Niué (the Savage Island of Captain Cook) and a large number of the scattered islets in other parts have also been occupied by missionaries, and a mission vessel, the *John Williams*, is regularly employed for ministering to the needs of the native teachers and communicating with all the stations.

Work in New Zealand had also so far advanced sixty years ago, that though it has passed through some troubled experiences since then, the missions of the Church Missionary Society and of the Wesleyans have been transformed into strong self-supporting native churches.

Two additional missionary movements have been begun within the period under review, both of them of peculiar interest.   In 1847 Bishop Selwyn of New Zealand found an opportunity of paying a visit to a portion of the South Sea Islands, which had somehow been included in his diocese.   He went as chaplain of *H.M.S. Dido*, and after visiting Tonga, Samoa, and Aneityum, went on to the Melanesian Islands, which he found entirely uncared for.   The sandal-wood trader, the trader in *bêche de mer*, and the labour vessel had found out these places, but no missionary was at work.   His

heart was greatly stirred, and he determined to commence a mission.   Unfortunately there was a perfect
babel of languages, every small island apparently having
a language of its own.   The climate also was exceedingly unhealthy.   He came to the conclusion that the
only hope of doing satisfactory work would be by
getting boys away from the islands, training them, and
sending them back to their own people.   This was the
origin of the settlement afterwards made on Norfolk
Island.   In 1849 he entered upon the work, and obtained
for the purpose the *Undine*, a small vessel of 20 tons,
in which he made voyages amounting to more than
20,000 miles.   In 1850 he visited Sydney for counsel
with the five Australian bishops.   One result of this
consultation was the formation of the Australasian
Board of Missions, in connection with the Episcopal
Church.   A new and larger vessel, the *Border Maid*,
was purchased, and this was in turn superseded in
1855 by the *Southern Cross*.   From 1857 the work
was in the hands of John Coleridge Patteson, who in
1861 was consecrated Bishop of Melanesia, and who
gave himself to his difficult task with the self-sacrificing
devotion and the contagious enthusiasm of a beautifully
consecrated life.   He gained a wonderful influence among
the natives, and made the settlement on Norfolk Island
a great success.   His great linguistic powers were shown
in his extraordinary mastery of the languages of the
islands, several of which he reduced to writing.   The
respect in which he was held by the wild men with
whom he had to do was shown in a strange and grim
yet touching fashion by the circumstances of his death.
A labour vessel cruising among the islands had been
disguised by paint and rigging to appear like the
Southern Cross, in order that natives might be induced
to come on board.   In this guise the vessel had called
at Nukapu and had kidnapped and carried off five of the

islanders.   Not long after, the *Southern Cross* arrived at the island, with the bishop on board.   "There were seen four canoes hovering to windward, and not approaching the schooner as usual, so the boat was lowered and the bishop pulled toward the shore.   The tide was low, and the boat could not cross the reef; so he got into a canoe manned by two chiefs whom he knew, and was taken ashore.   In a short time a flight of poisoned arrows was directed at the boat, and the Rev. J. Atkin and two natives were mortally wounded.   The boat went back to the ship, and, returning with the rising tide, pulled in to the lagoon, her party having grave forebodings as to the fate of the bishop.   There they found his murdered body laid, not without care and reverence, in a canoe which was drifting towards the ship.   A native mat tied round the neck and ankles covered the body, and into the folds of the breast a palm branch was thrust, with five knots tied in it.   The old law of retaliation had prompted the deed, and the five knots showed that the five friends who had been carried into captivity fraudulently had been avenged."[1]

The regulation of the labour traffic and the punishment of evildoers by the British Government has prevented such tragedies from happening again.   The Melanesian Mission has progressed steadily.   Printing-presses are set up in each group of islands, and native catechists trained at Norfolk Island are already at work among their own countrymen.

Within the Melanesian area in the South Seas is a group of beautiful volcanic islands, thirty in number, known as the New Hebrides.   Captain Cook's descriptions of the natives and their customs are among the most interesting parts of his journals.   John Williams was very anxious to introduce the gospel to these islands, and it was on a visit to Erromanga in 1839 that

[1] Tucker, *English Church in other Lands*, p. 107.

the greatest pioneer missionary of the Pacific was murdered with his companion, the Rev. John Harris. After the death of Williams, the missionary ship called again and again at one or other of the islands, Aneityum, Fotuna, Aniwa, Tanna, and Erromanga. Messrs. Turner and Nisbet from Samoa also attempted to reside at Tanna, but every attempt to come into permanent friendly relations with the natives seemed to be in vain. Several of the teachers were murdered; the others, with the two European missionaries, had to flee. The work done, however, was not in vain. In 1848 the Presbyterian Church of Nova Scotia sent out the Rev. John Geddie, who landed on Aneityum. He found forty-five persons ready to gather for worship on his first Sunday there, and his work began to be blessed from the outset. The history of the succeeding years at Aneityum is summed up in the inscription on the memorial tablet to Mr. Geddie at Anelgahat, the place which had been his missionary home: "When he landed in 1848, there were no Christians here, and when he died in 1872, there were no heathen".

The first converts on Aneityum became the pioneers on the other islands, and after a long hard struggle the group is now included among those which are christianized. What sacrifice, endurance, and faith were required for work on those islands has been described in the autobiography of the Rev. J. G. Paton.

The New Hebrides Mission is carried on under the guidance of a committee representing the Presbyterian Church in Canada, the Free Church of Scotland, and the Presbyterian Churches in the Australasian Colonies.

The latest extension of missionary enterprise in the South Seas is to the great island of New Guinea. In 1871 the London Missionary Society commenced work among the wild Papuans on the south coast of New Guinea, by means of eight native teachers from the

Loyalty Islands.   They were conveyed to Darnley Island by the Revs. A. W. Murray and S. M'Farlane, and settled there and on the islands of Dauan and Saibai.   Thirteen additional native missionaries arrived in the following year.   In 1874 a settlement was effected on the mainland at Port Moresby by the Rev. W. G. Lawes.   Since then the mission, largely through the wonderful influence of the Rev. James Chalmers, has spread from point to point along the southern coast from Torres Straits to East Cape.   The climate has proved very trying even to the South Sea Islanders, many of whom have died of fever and other troubles.   Some have suffered from the treachery of the natives.   But the zeal and enthusiasm of the converts in the South Seas has proved equal to the constant demands made upon them.   Upwards of 350 men and women from various parts of the London Missionary Society's South Sea Mission have given themselves to work in New Guinea, and many of them have done splendid service.

In 1892 two other societies entered the field.   The Anglican Mission, promoted by the Board of Missions in Australasia, has undertaken the evangelization of the northern coast of the peninsula, from East Cape to the boundaries of the German territory.   The Wesleyans have commenced a mission in the Louisiade group of islands at the east end of New Guinea.   This mission is making remarkable progress.

A hasty survey, such as is now completed, of the many and varied fields of labour entered into by the missionary enterprise of the Christian Church in Great Britain may be found useful by those who desire to have before them, in a compact form, a record of what has been done and attempted by the various sections of the Church.   It requires, however, a more detailed study of the various directions in which this great and many-sided work has been developed in order to gain any true idea of the real greatness and complexity of the missionary problem. Some idea of the kind of work that has been attempted will be found in the following pages.

Chapter IV.

Education.

In no direction has the gradual development and expansion of missionary policy been more marked than in the education of the young in its relation to missionary effort. From the outset, the necessity for giving a certain amount of education to converts and the children of converts has been recognized with remarkable unanimity by all missionary workers. This was at first done in most cases not so much with a view to the intellectual development of the converts, as from a religious reason. The first object sought in teaching was that the learners might be able to read the Scriptures, and might take an intelligent part in the simple Christian services established for their benefit. The religious aim was in many mission fields helped by the fact that the only reading book available was a translation of one of the Gospels, or of some other portion of Scripture. For instance, in the New Guinea Mission of the London Missionary Society, the one reading book for the scholars in its hundred schools has, until lately, been the Gospel according to St. Mark, which has been translated by the missionaries into nine of the languages used on that many-tongued coast. Now, at length, as the mission becomes more thoroughly consolidated and developed, elementary reading books on general subjects of interest to the people are being prepared. Something like this is probably the history of every mission which is still in the pioneer stage.

Side by side with this general recognition of the necessity for some elementary instruction for all, came the need for giving some special training to those who were to be employed as preachers and teachers. This has been felt even by those who have held the most extreme views of the influence of the Holy Spirit as the teacher as well as the inspirer of all true workers. Consequently, in every mission some provision has been made, sooner or later, for the instruction of native workers. The educational policy of the various missionary organizations begins to take shape consciously or unconsciously at this point. On the necessity for providing suitable training for the native ministry all are agreed who believe in a stated ministry. The requirements of the ministry necessarily differ somewhat under different conditions of life, and the ideas of the kind and quality of the training required have developed with the growth of the general standard of knowledge among the Christian communities. In the early days of every mission, each missionary sought such native helpers as he could get, and gave them such training as he had the time or the ability to give them. But that stage has long since passed in almost every mission field. Nearly all the larger societies have long since established training institutions for the native ministry in every important mission, and many of these institutions have grown educationally until they have become fairly entitled to the name of colleges. The Fourah Bay College of the Church Missionary Society in Sierra Leone was among the earliest of these schools of divinity, having been founded in 1827. It has been affiliated to Durham University since 1876, and between that date and 1891 twenty-seven of its students had taken the B.A. degree. Passing to the opposite side of

Central Africa, and to a mission comparatively young, it will be found that the theological classes of the Livingstonia Institution on Lake Nyassa, which have only been in full operation for a couple of years, aim at preparing the native workers in that mission very thoroughly. The students "have been striving earnestly to attain such a mastery of English as would enable them with greater facility to grasp the various subjects forming part of their course. With the Rev. Mr. Henderson they studied Introduction to the Books of the Old Testament, the Books of Proverbs and Ecclesiastes, exegesis of a number of the Psalms, and systematic theology. With Dr. Laws they studied Introduction to the New Testament, especially the Pastoral Epistles, exegesis, and the First Epistle to Timothy, and Church history to the close of the third century. The comparison between the conditions of life in the early Christian Church, and the state of things following the advent of the gospel to their own country, proved most interesting to the students; while the planting and development of Churches in the midst of heathenism, and the difficulties these Churches had to meet and overcome, have had far more reality to them than to students at home. In exegesis the Scriptures in English and the vernacular are used." (*Report of the Livingstonia Mission*, Free Church of Scotland, 1899.)

The curriculum of study at the Lovedale Theological School of the same mission in South Africa, is, as might be expected in a much older mission, much more complete. The course occupies three years, it provides for the exegetical and critical study of the Scripture, gives the students a careful grounding in systematic and pastoral theology, in apologetics, and in Church history.

The college at Antananarivo connected with the London Missionary Society's mission in Madagascar has now been in existence thirty years. The course of study occupies five years, and the students receive instruction in grammar, logic, mathematics, history, and science, in addition to a careful training in the study of the Bible, in systematic theology, homiletics, and Church history. In the same society's Training Institution at Malua, Samoa, an equally thorough course of training is given. The Rev. G. Turner, LL.D., one of the founders, and for many years one of the tutors, gave an account of his work at the General Conference on Missions in London in 1888, in which he said: "The course of instruction is in the vernacular, and embraces reading, writing, arithmetic, geometry, natural philosophy, geography, geology, natural history, Scripture exposition, systematic and pastoral theology, and Church history. We have a class for the English language, in which *Young Samoa* is especially interested. To help in these classes we have nine printed text-books, embracing arithmetic, the first book of Euclid, geography, natural philosophy, natural history, a doctrinal catechism, Scripture history, Church history, pastoral theology, and popery. We have had a native assistant tutor for many years, who is most helpful in elementary branches, and in conducting classes in the absence of either of the missionary tutors. . . . Other works on Christian and educational literature have been printed, and are also in the hands of the students. There is a condensed commentary on the Old and New Testaments; eight volumes of notes, practical and expository, embracing the Book of Psalms, Matthew, Mark, John, the Acts of the Apostles, Romans, Galatians, the Epistles to Timothy, Titus, and Hebrews, together with the Epistles of James, Peter, John, and Jude; two volumes of sketches of sermons; a translation of Bunyan, and of the *Peep of Day*; a Scripture concordance; a Bible dictionary; and some other works; making in all thirty-two volumes, and containing an aggregate of ten thousand pages in

the Samoan dialect.   We have also a grammar and
dictionary of the language in English, a second edition
of which was published by Messrs. Trubner, of London,
ten years ago." (*Report of the Missionary Conference*,
London, 1888.   Vol. ii. pp. 210–11.)

The mission of the Presbyterian Church of England
in China has from the beginning given much attention
to the training of the native ministry, and has now *four*
theological colleges.   They have still as students some
men who have come out of heathenism in mature life,
and for whom a special course of study is required, but
an increasing number of young men are now being
admitted who have received a fairly complete elementary
and secondary education in the Congregational Primary
Schools in the country, and in the High School at the
mission centre.   "The regular course for these men
occupies four years, each consisting of two terms, one of
four, and one of five months.   During this time they again
read through the Chinese text of the whole Bible, practising translation from the literary language into the
vernacular, and making a more special exegetical study
of selected books, both from the Old Testament and
the New.   They also study Church history, the elements
of systematic (or rather Biblical) theology, keep up and
extend their knowledge of arithmetic, geography, and
general history, receive some instruction in physical
science and astronomy, and practise composition and
the preparation of sermons."

Illustrations of this kind might be multiplied from
every part of the mission field, and from the work of
every society.   The Episcopal Church, the various
Presbyterian missions, the Baptists, the Wesleyans,
and other Methodist societies, and the London Missionary Society, have all recognized with increasing
clearness the growing need for an educated native
ministry, and are striving to supply that need in accord-

ance with the special requirements of different countries and different conditions of civilization.

The more general question of the education of the young as part of the duty of the Christian missionary stands in an altogether different category from that of the training of native evangelists and pastors. The training of the ministry seems to be, from any point of view, a matter of direct and primary importance to those who are expecting to see a self-supporting, self-propagating, indigenous Christianity developed as the result of their missionary effort. In regard to the duty of the Church to provide for the education of the young in the mission field, there is room for a very marked difference of opinion, not only as to the point to which the missionary teacher may legitimately go in teaching without being unfaithful to his great commission to preach the gospel, but also as to the persons who are to be allowed to share in the advantages of such instruction as is given. Is the school to be confined to the children of converts and those under Christian influence, or may the children of the heathen share in its advantages? Is the duty of the true missionary limited in regard to education to what may be described as primary school work? Is the teacher inferior to the preacher as a missionary? Or is the duty of the missionary to do all in his power in every direction to elevate the people among whom he is labouring materially, socially, and intellectually, as well as spiritually? The divergence of view indicated by these questions has become more distinct as the work of missions has become more thoroughly organized. There are some missions in which education as a missionary duty is completely subordinated to the oral proclamation of the gospel, and in which, therefore, no serious effort appears to be attempted to make the instruction of the young a definite feature of the work in which the missionaries are engaged. In a second and larger group of missionary organizations the progress of work has led to a much wider view of the Christian commission, and of the responsibility of those who carry the gospel to the heathen towards those who are gathered into the Church of Christ by their instrumentality. Often very slowly, and to a large extent unconsciously, the conviction has been formed, and has become more or less clearly defined, that, in the circumstances of the present day, Christian responsibility towards the converts from heathenism has not ended when they have been taught the rudiments of the gospel and provided with the Scriptures. The spirit of the great Christian commission has not been fully carried out until the new Christian communities have been set on their feet intellectually as well as spiritually, and fitted to face the difficulties and to meet the responsibilities which have been created for them largely by their contact with the world of Western life.

At this point there has been a further divergence. There are many who recognize in a liberal spirit their duty towards the native Christian community, but who hesitate to expend money, or time, or missionary force upon the provision of educational advantages for those who are not Christians. The directly and definitely religious results of educational work in producing conversions are necessarily so small that they feel that a missionary is not in his legitimate sphere, and the funds raised for missionary purposes are not being properly applied, when they are employed in the advancement of general education. On the other hand, it is maintained that under certain conditions the school and the college are the most efficient means that can be used for convincing the reason and influencing the affections, and thus preparing the way for the triumph of faith in Christ. Educational methods have, therefore, been boldly adopted as one of the most important means of evangelization.

The extent to which this branch of missionary effort is carried necessarily varies considerably according to circumstances. There is a very great difference in the value of education in different parts of the world. In the South Sea Islands it is still to a large extent an ornamental accomplishment, apparently leading no-where, and bringing to the educated man no practical advantage unless he is going into the ministry. In India, on the other hand, education is the golden gate which leads to all honour and profit. While in China, until quite recently, all Western knowledge has actually been at a discount, except in some of the principal treaty ports, where a limited number were enabled thereby to find lucrative employment in foreign mer-cantile offices.

Again, in some parts of the world it has become increasingly evident that the earlier efforts to educate by the cultivation of the intellect alone were made on wrong lines. Where uncivilized races are brought into close connection with white men in the same com-munity, they have to learn to be useful members of a society which is regulated by very different condi-tions from those which they have been accustomed to. Under such conditions technical and industrial training is of greater value than a knowledge of grammar and geography. Next to the inculcation of moral principle, the best service that can be rendered to many races is to train the young in habits of sustained and intelli-gent industry and to instruct them in useful handicrafts. The result of such training is not only an increase of self-respect, but also of the respect of others.

The course which education has taken in connection with missionary work has thus varied considerably in different parts of the mission field. There has, however, been a steady and a remarkable extension of effort during the last sixty years.   Let it be remembered that the whole apparatus of education has had to be created by the missionaries from its most elementary stages upwards, and that this has had to be done in a multitude of languages.   In Africa, America, Madagascar and all the islands of the seas, these languages had first to be reduced to writing before the first reading lesson could be given, and every step in the upward progress in knowledge has had to be created by the missionary teachers by means either of translations of English books or by original preparation.   This being the case, it is surprising to learn what has been accomplished in this direction even in the less advanced mission fields.   The statement by Dr. Turner of Samoa, already quoted, is an illustration from one of the small and simpler missions of the kind of work which has been required in all parts of the mission field before education can be carried on to any extent.   It is true not only in the countries where the language has been reduced to writing for the first time by the missionaries, but also in lands like India and China, which possess a literature of their own.   When Dr. Wilson of Bombay established the Ambrolie English School, which afterwards became the General Assembly's institution in Bombay, "books as well as teachers had to be created for it".   The puerility and impurity of Indian literature has made it impossible to adopt it for reading purposes in mission schools, while in China the idea of the nature of education which is current is so utterly worthless from a Western point of view, that new school-books were required from the very beginning.   It is no exaggeration to say that the education of a large part of the world is entirely dependent on missionary effort.   It is now beginning to be evident that by these efforts the bondage and degradation of past ignorance are being

broken and removed on a scale which is rapidly producing a silent but far-reaching revolution. Already it
is manifest by many individual proofs that the degraded
races are in their present depressed condition not from
any inherent inferiority in brain capacity, but as the
result of circumstances which may be corrected. Given
peace, freedom, a new intellectual stimulus, and opportunity, and they will prove themselves to be no unworthy
members of the brotherhood of civilized nations.

The attempt to describe in detail the extent and
variety of the educational effort which is now being
carried on by the various British missionary societies
would speedily degenerate into very uninteresting tables
of figures. The original simple primary school is found
wherever a missionary is found, and in every permanent
sub-station where a native helper is at work. But as
the work progressed and the intelligence of the people
grew, the primary school was long ago followed by the
second-grade school, the high school, and the college.
The demand for teachers, and for improvement in the
quality of the teaching, has led to the commencement of
normal training classes, and ultimately in the larger
missions to the establishment of well-equipped normal
schools.

In the Cape Colony the students from the Presbyterian institutions at Lovedale and Blythswood, the
Wesleyan school at Healdtown, the Primitive Methodist
school at Aliwal North, and the Church of England
schools at Grahamstown and Keiskamma compete
with Europeans in the Government examinations for
the teachers' certificates, and are able to hold their
own and take high positions in the lists. In other
regions where there is no such competitive test similar
training is being given, and every year witnesses fresh
efforts to increase the efficiency of the teaching and to
raise the general standard of education.

The importance of industrial and technical teaching has during recent years become very generally recognized, not only in countries where uncivilized peoples come into increasing contact with Europeans, but also where depressed classes require to be lifted up into a position of healthy self-support and self-respect. In Africa especially, industrial schools have taken a very important place in mission work. The Universities Mission at Zanzibar, the Blantyre Mission of the Church of Scotland, the Livingstonia Mission of the Free Church of Scotland, the Tanganyika Mission of the London Missionary Society, the Baptists on the Congo, the United Presbyterian Calabar Mission, the Church Missionary Society on the Lower Niger and at Taveta in East Africa, have all commenced industrial training; and their pupils are already proving themselves able to do a large amount of useful work in brick-making and in building, carpentering and joinery, printing, &c. Farther south this branch of education has been developed most thoroughly and satisfactorily at several important schools in the Cape Colony and in Kaffraria. The most important and successful of these schools are those of the Episcopal Mission at Grahamstown and St. Mark's Station, Keiskamma, and the two Presbyterian schools at Blythswood and Lovedale. A recent visitor to Grahamstown reported, after visiting the industrial school: "The apprentices in this school turn out a variety of useful articles, for which there is constant demand, such as stools, tables, hanging shelves, hanging cupboards, corner cupboards, clothes-horses, screens, camp-tables, ladders, wheel-barrows, washstands, steps, frames, &c. But they also do first-class work. They made the chancel screen for the Grahamstown Cathedral, and were making a canopy for the choir stalls when I was there." The work at St. Mark's, Keiskamma, is on a larger and more important scale than this: the school has become the centre of a village, and wagon-making, blacksmithing, and tinsmith's work are done by the pupils. Lovedale is a still more remarkable centre of varied industries, and has become one of the sights of South Africa for those who are interested in efforts for the elevation of the people.

The establishment of boarding-schools for the children of converts was long objected to by many on the general principle that it would tend to pauperize and at the same time to weaken the sense of parental responsibility. This objection has naturally been most strongly felt by the managing committees in Great Britain, but it has also been recognized by many of the missionaries in the field. Gradually, however, the practical difficulties of converts living in the midst of heathenism have been more clearly recognized, and the necessity for making provision for the separation, where practicable, of the children, and especially of the girls, from the polluting influences of the life around them, have been admitted. Moreover, the converts themselves have become increasingly alive to the value of such provision as is furnished by the boarding-school, and have in many cases been willing to pay for the privilege of having their children thus cared for, so that many schools have become largely self-supporting. In every part of the mission field, and by almost every society, such schools are now regarded as a necessity.

The most striking illustration of the work that has been done by Christian missions in connection with education is to be found in British India. In no other part of the mission field is there anything to compare with it in extent or in fulness of development. Nowhere else have the great principles which should guide missionary societies in relation to education been so hotly debated.

It would not be correct to say that India owes the educational provision it now enjoys to missionary effort, yet it would be altogether misleading and inaccurate to treat lightly the missionary element in any study of the history and present condition of education in India. Thousands of indigenous vernacular schools were in existence in the country before any provision was made either by the East India Company or by missionaries. These schools were, however, of very little value except as places for the acquisition of the most elementary knowledge of reading. They were entirely confined to boys, and were entirely devoted to teaching Hinduism, or were attached to Mohammedan mosques. The earliest provision for the instruction of the natives in any systematic manner in Western knowledge was made by Carey and his companions, and by Forsyth of the London Missionary Society, in 1798. The Serampore missionaries had before the end of 1816 given instruction in their schools to more than 10,000 heathen children. The schools established by Mr. Forsyth numbered thirty at the end of the same year, with an attendance of 2600 scholars.

In consequence of the growth of these mission schools, the School Book Society was formed in Calcutta in 1817. In the following year the Calcutta School Society was established, "to improve indigenous schools, to found new ones, and to prepare native teachers for the work of education".

Similarly the Bombay Native Instruction Society was formed in 1815.

Though the Hindu College in Calcutta was established by the Government in 1817, no attempt was made to improve and extend elementary education for many years, except by private Christian philanthropy, and by the missionary societies. Several years before any Government scheme was developed, two men went out as missionaries to India, who had immense influence on the course of education. One was the Rev. Alexander Duff, the other was the Rev. John Wilson.

Alexander Duff was the first missionary of the Church of Scotland. He was sent out in 1829 in consequence of the decision of the General Assembly to commence mission work in India. That decision was the result of the recommendation of a special committee appointed to consider the whole subject of the relation of the Church to missions, and it took its form from the nature of the recommendation made to it. The committee advised that in the first instance one of the British provinces in India should be the field of labour, and that the work should be on educational lines by the establishment of a central school under the direction of an ordained minister of the Church, with branch schools; that Christianity should be prominently advocated in the curriculum of study, and that in addition the Principal should seek opportunities of preaching. Duff landed in Calcutta in 1830, after a most adventurous voyage of nearly eight months. He promptly made himself acquainted with the situation, and came to the conclusion that English should be the medium through which instruction should be given. He opened his school with five pupils on July 12, 1830, and speedily had it crowded. This was the beginning of a new educational policy in India. Previously, Sanscrit and the other classic languages of India had been used exclusively as the medium of instruction for students. Henceforth, though only after a prolonged and vigorous controversy, English became the language of collegiate study.

In the same year that Duff landed in Calcutta, the Rev. John Wilson went to Bombay as a missionary of the Edinburgh or Scottish Missionary Society, and speedily won for himself a unique place in the respect and affection of all sections in the community. Like

Duff, he also gave his attention at once to education, and established schools, which soon grew into large and influential educational establishments. Both these great workers exerted so direct and powerful a Christian influence that their teaching proved a most effectual form of ministry. Some of the finest men who have served the native Church in India were the fruits of their educational ministry. In 1837 the Church of Scotland commenced a mission in Madras, and established a school there which was the forerunner of the Christian College, the greatest and most successful educational institution in India at the present time.

During the next twenty years the Indian Government, which was compelled in 1833 on the renewal of its charter to spend £100,000 a year on education, gave itself chiefly to the work of encouragement of learning by liberal support of the colleges at the cost of the education of the poor. The missionary societies, on the other hand, were steadily endeavouring, so far as means and opportunity permitted, to extend their work among the ignorant masses. The Report of the Education Commission appointed in 1882 refers very candidly and sympathetically "to the important part taken by missionary societies in originating and carrying on modern culture in India. In going over the different provinces it is shown that in almost every instance the missionary had preceded the Government in setting up schools of every kind; and the great service rendered by them in female education is frankly and gracefully acknowledged." Such sentences as the following are frequently found: "As noticed in paragraph 96 of the despatch of 1854, Southern India owes much of its educational progress to the efforts of missionary societies. . . . It is estimated that in 1854 about 30,000 boys were being educated in schools conducted by missionary societies in Southern India." (*Abstract and Analysis of the Report of the Education Commission in India.* Hamilton, Adams, & Co., 6*s*.)

In 1854 came the now celebrated despatch by Sir Charles Wood, by which the educational policy of the Government received a new direction and a new impulse. The object of the despatch was defined to be to encourage by Government assistance "the more extended and systematic promotion of general education in India". It recognizes that much has been done with limited means for the education of the few, and that very high results have been attained. But it asserts the wish of the Government to see the advantages of education widely extended. It introduces the system of grants in aid to all schools and colleges on the results of their secular teaching, and irrespective of their religious position, and it anticipates the time when, as the result of the development of private enterprise by such grants in aid, the direct connection of the State with education by the maintenance of Government colleges and schools will entirely cease. The Imperial Government have never varied from this position, and have restated it again and again, but the tendency among those who are administering the Education Department in India has been in favour of upholding the old system at the expense of the new. The friends of missions in Great Britain formed themselves into a "Council on Education in India", and made representations to the Marquis of Ripon on the eve of his departure for India in 1880, and to Her Majesty's Government in April, 1881, which led to the appointment of a very strong Commission of Enquiry, the largest and most important that ever sat in India. The instructions to this Commission declared "that its duty should be to enquire into the manner in which effect had been given to the despatch of 1854, and to suggest such methods as it might think desirable, with a view to more completely carrying out the policy therein laid down ".

The result of this progressive policy has been that
India now enjoys the benefit of a system of State-aided
as well as State-superintended education. Hindus,
Mohammedans, Parsees, and Christians are all alike
encouraged to establish schools and colleges, and to
earn grants in aid by educational proficiency in secular
subjects. Municipal funds are in many cases being
employed to carry on Anglo-vernacular schools, and the
Government itself continues to maintain colleges and
schools for purely secular teaching.

The missionary societies have not been slow in avail-
ing themselves of the encouragement thus afforded, and
have developed their educational efforts in many directions and with great success. The Church Missionary
Society, *e.g.*, has "9 divinity schools, 11 normal and
training institutions, 21 high schools and colleges, 89
Anglo-vernacular schools, 47 orphanages and boarding-
schools, and 1137 vernacular schools". The Free Church
of Scotland has only *three* colleges, situated at Calcutta,
Bombay, and Madras, but these three are conspicuous
among all educational institutions in India for the
quality of their teaching and the large percentage of
university honours that fall to their share. The Society
for the Propagation of the Gospel, the Church of Scotland, the Wesleyans, and the London Missionary
Society have all been active in the cause of education,
and their colleges and schools are giving instruction to
many thousands. Not only are these missionary educational establishments aided by grants from Government,
but they receive from the pupils fees which suffice in all
the more advanced schools and the colleges, with the
Government grants, to meet all the local expenses of
education. The result of this very properly is that the
cost of education is borne by those who receive it rather
than by the supporters of missions in Great Britain.

The necessity for such educational work in connection

with missions in India is twofold. In the first place, the Government in its schools and colleges restricts itself absolutely to secular teaching. An attempt has recently been made to provide text-books on subjects of general morality, but even these are supposed to be purged of any directly religious sanctions. The effect has been much more serious than can have been imagined by those who inaugurated the secular system. Dr. M'Namara of Calcutta, speaking to the Medical School of Westminster Hospital, in October, 1883, is reported to have said: " Our system of education has broken down all faith in religion, and the outcome of a purely secular training has developed gross materialism and rank secularism ". This serious statement embodies the concurrent testimony of many thoughtful observers, and indicates one of the reasons why missionary societies feel it to be necessary to occupy themselves with the work of education. In the mission colleges and schools the Bible and Christian teaching are an essential part of the curriculum, and the young who thus come under the influence of the missionaries pass forth into active life with at least a clear knowledge of the foundations of Christian morality.

Another reason for the maintenance of this educational work is that it furnishes the only opportunity of reaching the most influential class in Hindu and Mohammedan society. India under British rule is rapidly passing through great changes, and the most potent factor of change is the educational system, which is opening the door of Western knowledge and, above all, of English ideas on all subjects to the young, and tempting them to enter in by making education the avenue to office and honour. The new India of the next generation is rapidly being formed under these educational influences, and the future of India will depend upon the moral stand-point of the generation thus growing up. Yet this is a class which cannot be reached by open-air preaching, and which will not enter mission halls. If they are suffered to grow up under the purely negative influences of a secular education they will be quite beyond reach when they have grown to maturity. The teacher's desk and the professor's chair furnish the only means of evangelizing them, and they are available at the most susceptible and formative period of life. Confessions of faith in Christ are not numerous among school-boys or even students who live in heathen homes, but every year is bringing increasing evidence that the best men in the Indian churches, the leaders of Christian thought among the native Christian community, and the true hope of India are gathered from the students in the mission colleges.

Chapter V.

Special Developments—Literature.

No part of the missionary enterprise is more necessary or laborious than the production of a Christian literature in the various languages of mankind; and though astonishing progress has been made in many ways during the past sixty years, the demand for enlarged and systematic effort is one of the urgent needs of to-day. "Missionary literature", says Dr. Cust, "is perhaps one of the most marvellous phenomena that the world has ever seen. A language that a few years previously had never been committed to writing, and which had not developed words to express abstract ideas, is modulated by skilled hands so as to answer all the requirements of the highest civilization, and the natives themselves, no longer savages, are trained to aid in the translation and in the setting up of types."

No less wonderful is the success with which written languages, which have long been the literary vehicles of great civilizations, have been made to express the highest conceptions of Christianity and to become the channels by which its exalted teaching may be conveyed to vast and unenlightened masses. In this chapter an attempt will be made to give in rough outline some idea of what has been accomplished by British agencies during the past sixty years.

The vast scope of the work and its immense labour may be imagined from the number and variety of the languages and dialects in which it has been conducted. The British and Foreign Bible Society's Report for 1838 contains a list of 136 different versions; the same society's report for 1898 gives 351, but this falls short of the entire number of tongues in which the Scriptures now speak, which is not 351, but 400.[1] This large figure includes, of course, all parts of the world, so that some deduction must be made for the European versions, which do not come within the scope of this book; and a further deduction must be made for the valuable work done by non-British societies. After due allowance has been made, we shall be within the mark in saying that the past sixty years have witnessed at least the beginnings of Christian literature in 200 languages through the labours of British foreign mission agencies. There are now outside Europe[2] complete Bibles[3] in 69 tongues spoken in the mission fields here under review, of which 20 were completed before 1837, 14 had been begun before that year and have been completed since, and 35 are entirely new. Of the 49 Bibles which fall within our period, only 13 are non-British, so that the British

[1] See "Four Hundred Tongues", by Rev. J. G. Watt, M.A., *Bible Society Reporter*, February, 1899.

[2] Turkey is omitted as being so largely an American mission field.

[3] See "The Bibles of the World", by Rev. J. G. Watt, M.A., *Bible Society Reporter*, October, 1896.

addition to foreign missionary complete Bibles in the sixty years is 36.[1]

Following the same classification, we find outside Europe 79 complete New Testaments,[2] of which 17 were in existence before 1837, 5 were begun before that year and have been completed since, and 57 are entirely new. Of the 62 New Testaments, 15 are non-British, and the remaining 47 are the product of British agencies. To have translated, revised, printed, and published 36 versions of the whole Bible and 47 versions of the whole New Testament is no small achievement, to say nothing of the promising beginnings which are being every year enlarged in some other 100 tongues.

This immense work could not have been accomplished without the continuous and unstinted help of the British and Foreign Bible Society, which, in addition to its own extensive efforts to circulate the Scriptures,[3] has in the vast majority of cases not only printed the versions without cost to the societies making use of them, but has constantly aided their production by supporting missionaries when engaged in translation work and by bringing together the most able revisers and harmonizing their labours. Far beyond the achievements of all other Bible societies, British and foreign put together, are those of this "cosmopolitan and international" society, which last year circulated in all languages no less than 4,387,152 Bibles, Testaments, and portions, making its total issues since its formation in 1804, 155½ millions. Its pre-eminence is so marked that we feel justified in

[1] Four of these, viz. the Eskimo, Acra, Ashanti, and Sesuto, are reckoned as British because they were printed and published (with the usua lliberal help of the society to translators and revisers) by the British and Foreign Bible Society. The translators belonged to non-British societies.

[2] See "Complete New Testaments", by Rev. J. G. Watt, M.A., *Bible Society Reporter*, October, 1897.

[3] See page 169 for particulars of distribution by colporteurs and Bible-women, &c.

describing it in the remainder of this chapter as *The Bible Society*.

Next to The Bible Society, on account of the variety and importance of its missionary literature, comes the Religious Tract Society, which is now celebrating its centenary. In addition to its labours at home, this society has been conspicuous for its foreign missionary zeal, and by its publications, which rise from the little hand-bill and Scripture pictures to the commentary on Scripture or to the Bible itself, has generously helped all missionary societies. In 1837 it was employing 105 languages; in 1897 no less than 229, 166 of which are used in the foreign mission field. Last year its issues from foreign depots (including Europe) and societies more or less directly connected with it and assisted by grants of money or paper were estimated at 20,000,000. One of its special and most valuable contributions has been the issue of the *Pilgrim's Progress* in 91 languages, of which 60 are spoken in heathen lands.

A good deal in the publishing and preparation of Christian literature has also been effected by the Society for the Promotion of Christian Knowledge, which is now 200 years old. It describes itself as the Bible and Prayer-book Society of the Church of England, though The Bible Society issues a far greater number of Bibles for use in Church of England missions. Its yearly circulation of Bibles and Prayer-books, or portions of them, in seventy-five different languages exceeds half a million. Grants of money are also made to Church of England missions for the production of books in vernacular languages abroad. The National Bible Society of Scotland, formed in 1861, in addition to its work among British peoples, has issued or been directly helpful in the issue of the Scriptures in fifteen heathen tongues.

From these bewildering figures we pass to a brief

review of the chief results of the past sixty years in the
various fields, and begin with China, the land in which
the greatest importance is assigned to our subject, and
the *literati* rank next to the emperor in dignity and
power.   The first Chinese version of the Bible, published
in 1822, came from the prolific mission press in Serampore, and was the work of Dr. Marshman.   The version
by Morrison and Milne, which was of much greater
value, appeared in 1823.   The Delegates' Version, which
is still the standard,[1] was prepared at the instance of the
Hong Kong Conference of all Protestant Missions in
1852.   The delegates were Medhurst, Stronach, and
Milne, of the London Missionary Society, and Bishop
Boone, Bridgman, and Culbertson, who were Americans,
and who withdrew after the completion of the New
Testament.   The New Testament was published in 1852,
and the Old Testament in 1855.   The language of this
version is Wenli (sometimes called High Wenli), the
standard written language of the Chinese.   The number
who can read it is estimated from 12,000,000 to
16,000,000,[2] most of whom will translate it into their
vernaculars.   Hence it is necessary to provide vernacular
versions in order that the masses of the people may be
furnished with the Scriptures and some approach to
uniformity obtained.   In the Mandarin colloquial, which
possesses a literature and is spoken by two-thirds of the
people, the New Testament translated by Medhurst
and Stronach was issued in 1856.   The New Testament
in Northern Mandarin was published in 1870, and the
whole Bible at a later date.   Few of the other Chinese

---

[1] Bishop Hoâre of Hong Kong says: "Thank God for the Delegates'
Version!   It is magnificent.   There has never been a translation made in
such good style, or that commends itself so well to the Chinese." (*Bible
Society Reporter*, November, 1898.)

[2] Pp. 37, 38, *China and Formosa*, the Story of the English Presbyterian
China Mission.   Rev. James Johnston.   London: Hazell, Watson, & Viney,
1898.

dialects appear in print except in some special cases, such as the dialogues of novels, comic or low literature, and the moral sermons appointed to be read in the provinces on classic texts. Since 1860 about a dozen colloquial or vernacular versions have been made, among which may be mentioned those of Foochow, Amoy and Formosa, Swatow, Canton, Hainan, Hakka, Kien Ning, Shanghai, and Ningpo. Most of these are in the romanized style,[1] which has overcome the difficulty, and in some cases the impossibility, of writing the dialects in Chinese characters, and has conferred the marvellous boon of enabling a Chinaman to learn to read in six months if he gives only half an hour a day to the task. Besides the foregoing, the New Testament and Psalms have been published in easy Wenli, and references and annotations have been variously supplied. There can be no doubt that further notes and comments are needed for Chinese readers if the Book is not to remain sealed. Considerable help has been given in this direction by the Introduction bound up with the Scripture portions issued by the National Bible Society of Scotland, and by the issue of Archdeacon Moule's *Introduction to the Bible*, 150,000 copies of which were circulated last year by the colporteurs of the British and Foreign Bible Society. Revision is proceeding here, as almost everywhere in the mission field, but so far the committee appointed in 1890 to prepare what might prove a standard union Bible for all China has not made much progress. A revision of the New Testament, however, has been made at Hong Kong.

Turning to other literature, we have to record equally great and successful labours. It is natural for much to have been done in the land of Pi Sheng, who about

---

[1] In 1895 the Royal Asiatic Society adopted a scheme for the transliteration of Asiatic languages, which has been approved by the leading missionary societies.

1000 A.D. invented movable type and printed books with it nearly 500 years before Gutenberg,[1] and where a daily newspaper — *The Peking Gazette* — has been published for 1000 years. It is, however, very difficult to collect anything like full particulars. The vastness of the efforts of missionaries and their native coadjutors may be estimated by a perusal of the list of publications down to 1866 given in Wylie's *Memorials of Protestant Missionaries to China*, and in Dr. Murdoch's *Report on Christian Literature in China*, published in 1882, and in the records of the various societies about to be mentioned. Printing-presses have been established by several of the societies, beginning with that of the London Missionary Society, which has done great service from 1818 to the present time. In 1860 it was transferred to the American Presbyterians. From this first press the New Testament of the Delegates' Version was issued in 1852, and a year or two later the million New Testaments, which were circulated through the empire at the time of the Taiping rebellion, the cost being subscribed through the efforts of the Rev. J. Angell James of Birmingham. The press of the National Bible Society of Scotland at Hankow is one of the most important now at work, and last year issued more than a million Christian books and tracts. It has published the fullest reference edition of the New Testament, and such popular and widely-circulated tracts as Dr. Griffith John's "Gate of Wisdom and Virtue" and "Leading the Family in the Right Way". From the beginning, tracts have been scattered far and wide, one of the earliest being Milne's "Two Friends, or Twelve Dialogues between a Worshipper of God and a Heathen". This remarkable treatise is still published and has passed

---

[1] *Dawn on the Hills of T'ang, or China as a Mission Field*, by Harlan P. Beach. Student Volunteer Missionary Union, London, 1898.

through more than a dozen editions.[1]   Since 1875 seven
tract societies have been established,[2] all of which are
generously helped and encouraged in their work by
the Religious Tract Society.   Two other societies call
for fuller mention.   From the School and Text-book
Committee, appointed by the China Mission Conference
of 1877, has come the Society for the Diffusion of
Christian and General Knowledge among the Chinese,
which was at first under the inspiration and direction
of the Rev. Dr. Williamson of the United Presbyterian
Church.   Latterly this agency has been revived and
reinforced, and is now admirably conducted by the Rev.
Timothy Richard.   The Baptist Missionary Society, to
which Mr. Richard belongs, has generously set him
apart for this work, in aid of which some of the other
missionary organizations give annual grants.   The aim
of the society is to change "the hostile attitude of the
Mandarins, the gentry and educated classes", and to
provide "a good supply of suitable literature so as to
strengthen the hands of the few reformers who do their
best and wish to be friendly".   It publishes two monthly
magazines, one of which is general and designed to
inform the rulers and students of China of what Christian
governments are doing for their peoples, and the other
endeavours to instruct the leaders of the native churches
in the progress of Christ's Kingdom in all parts of the
world.   Its publications on such subjects as *The Life of
Christ, Natural Theology, Civilization, The Benefits of
Christianity,* and *How to Support the Nations,* already
number more than 100, and it is intended to place one
of them in the hands of every civil mandarin down to
the rank of a country mayor.   Special attention is also

[1] Other British presses are at Ningpo (C.M.S.), Swatow (Presbyterian),
Kiukiang (W.M.S.), Taichow (C.I.M.), Peking (S.P.G.).—*Dawn on Hills
of T'ang,* p. 111.
[2] *The China Mission Handbook,* pp. 303-306 (American Presbyterian
Mission Press, Shanghai, 1896; and *Religious Tract Society Report,* 1898).

given to the distribution and sale of books among the students at the various centres of examination; and by means of this and other societies no less than 200,000 books and tracts were put into the hands of Chinese scholars last year.[1] As the needs of an examination centre can be met for £20, it ought not to be long before all the 200 centres are thus provided for, and books of real enlightenment placed in the hands of China's million students.

The Educational Association of China[2] aims at the publication of school-books suited for mission schools, the improvement of methods of teaching, and the general promotion of educational interests, and has been steadily at work during the past few years. The catalogue of books issued or approved by the association fully warrants its assertion that "there is no reason why a pupil in China cannot be given a general education through the medium of his own language which will be fully the equivalent of a college education in the home lands, and which will fit him for valuable service both in Church and State". Provision is thus being made for the great changes which are taking place in China. At the time of writing, the astonishing reforms promulgated by the emperor in the direction of Western learning have received a temporary check; but that a question on the difference between the flood mentioned in the Chinese classics and that believed in by Western people should be given as the subject for an essay at the Kiangsi Examination is of vast significance. No less wonderful is the publication by the *literati* of Hunan of an anti-foot-binding tract, endorsed by the Viceroy Chang Chih Tung, and since issued, with a preface by Dr. Griffith John, by the Central China Tract Society. Since 1895 considerable advance has been

---

[1] Rev. G. H. Bondfield, *Religious Tract Society Report*, 1898, p. 163.
[2] *China Mission Handbook*, pp. 311-313.

made in Chinese newspapers and magazines. In that year there were only 11 newspapers and 8 magazines and periodicals. Now there are at least 35 newspapers and as many magazines and periodicals. Of the latter, 10 are issued by missionary societies or in the interests of the Christian Church, while the rest, with few exceptions, are all healthy in tone and liberal in tendency.[1] Important steps have thus been taken towards the literary equipment of the Church in China, and though much remains to be done in the way of preparation and circulation of an effective literature it is gratifying to know that not less than two millions and a quarter of books and tracts, and upwards of a million portions of the Old and New Testaments, were scattered through China in 1897.[2]

Brief mention must be made of countries in proximity to China. The mission of Stallybrass, Swan, and Yuille (London Missionary Society) among the Buriats, a Mongol tribe living in Siberia, which was terminated through Russian hostility in 1841, left as its permanent work the whole Bible in Mongolian. Gilmour frequently came across copies of the New Testament from this version during his Mongolian labours (1870–1891), and describes it as quite serviceable in the various regions of Mongolia. In 1870 a Kalkas version of St. Matthew was published.

More than forty years ago the New Testament and parts of the Old were published in Thibetan. There are happy indications that great opportunities for their circulation are not far off, and The Bible Society reports (1898) that providential guidance is supplying the men who will answer the call that has been made for revision.

The hermit kingdom of Korea was provided with the New Testament through the labours of the Rev.

---

[1] Paper on Native Newspapers, Rev. Ernest Box, Shanghai.
[2] *Religious Tract Society Report*, 1898, p. 163.

John Ross (United Presbyterian Mission).   This version, which was printed in 1893, is already undergoing
revision.   A Korean tract society has begun the provision of a much-needed Christian literature, and the
forward movement is harmoniously carried on by the
British, American, and Scottish Bible Societies, with
valuable help from the Australian Presbyterian Society.

The Japanese, who have only been accessible to the
gospel since 1859, and among whom British missions
date from 1869, have undergone a remarkable development in late years, having put on with amazing quick-
ness the outward forms of Western civilization.   Their
right to claim more literary activity than any other
Asiatic people is evidenced by the fact that though
twenty years ago they had never issued a newspaper,
there are now dailies in Tokio and 700 periodicals
throughout the empire.[1]   The honour of beginning the
work lies with the Americans, of whom Dr. Hepburn
has been conspicuous in literary labours, and whose
influence in the translation of the Bible has been most
important.   A united committee, assisted by native
helpers, produced the New Testament in 1880 and the
Old Testament in 1888.   The New Testament has also
passed through two editions in the Roman character.
Among the translators Rev. P. K. Fyson, now Bishop
of Hokhaido, deserves honourable mention.   In 1897
the Rev. J. Batchelor (Church Missionary Society)
translated the New Testament into Ainu, the speech
of the aborigines in the northern island.   The usual
provision of devotional literature in hymn- and prayer-
books has been made, and in addition a vast mass of
other Christian publications has been issued.   The
effect of these and other agencies upon the general
literature of the country has been considerable, for "no
one", says the Rev. Tomoyoshi Murari, a graduate of

---

[1] Dennis, *Foreign Missions after a Century*, p. 67.

the Doshisha College, "who examines our papers and magazines for the last fifteen years can fail to recognize the fact that Christianity has been working among the nation like leaven, elevating the tone of her moral sentiments, and widening her horizon".[1] The Religious Tract Society reports a circulation of books and tracts amounting to 627,000.

Malaysia with its many nationalities and languages next claims attention. Singapore has become, especially of late years, a great centre of Bible distribution[2] in many languages: Malay, in both Arabic and Roman characters; Chinese, Javanese, Tamil, English, and Dutch. The Bible in Malay is chiefly the work of the Rev. B. P. Keasberry (London Missionary Society), who laboured in Singapore from 1845 to 1875. Portions of the Scriptures have also been issued in fifteen other tongues, amongst which the Gospels and Acts in Pagasinan, and St. Matthew, St. Mark, St. Luke, and the Acts in Tagalog, and St. Luke in Bicol, for use in the Philippines, are of special interest. The Society for the Propagation of the Gospel has published the Prayer-book and other devotional books in Malay.

Turning to India, we are confronted by the immense mass of religions, races, and languages which are brought together under that pregnant name. We must content ourselves in this vast field with mentioning the more considerable products. At the commencement of the Queen's reign important beginnings had been made in 55 Indian tongues. Since then translations have been produced in 30 additional dialects. These figures, however, give a most inadequate conception of the real progress made, as they take no account of the careful and constantly repeated

---

[1] *National Bible Society of Scotland Report*, 1897, p. 49.
[2] Edmonds' *Expansion of Bible Society, 1837–1897*, p. 35.

revisions which have been made in the chief Bibles.

In North India seven great Aryan languages are found, in all of which, except Sindhi and Panjabi, which have only the New Testament, the whole Bible is circulated. The extent of possible circulation will be seen in the figures given below.[1]

The Marathi Bible, which, with the Gujarati, owes much to Dr. John Wilson, was first published in 1847, since which time it has undergone two revisions. The Gujarati Bible, completed in 1832, has since been subjected to much revision, and at last (1896) been issued in a fairly satisfactory form through the efforts of the Irish Presbyterian Mission. In 1852 a Gujarati version of the New Testament was prepared for Parsees, with the help of Revs. Dhanjibhai Nauroji and Hormazdji Pestonji. The Hindi Bible takes us back again to the gigantic labours of Dr. Carey. Since his time it has been subjected to a succession of revisers, the result of whose labours were published in 1869. The Old Testament is now being retranslated, and will probably be published next year. The Urdu version presents a similar history. In 1811 the devoted Henry Martyn had translated the New Testament, but the Old Testament was not finished for more than thirty years. Since then various revisers have been at work. The New Testament, which has been completed by a committee of translators, among whom Dr. Weitbrecht (Church Missionary Society) takes a foremost place, will be shortly issued in Persian and Roman characters. The Bengali Bible is specially associated with Carey, Yates, Wenger, and Rouse, of the Baptist Missionary Society. The last-named reviser's work has recently been issued by The Bible Society contemporaneously with a student's

---

[1] Sindhi population 2 millions, Panjabi 14½ millions, Gujarati 9½ millions, Marathi 17 millions, Hindi with Urdu 83 millions, Bengali 39 millions, Uriya 7 millions (*Expansion of Bible Society, 1837–1897*, p. 41).

edition, with references, variant readings, and a broad margin. A committee is at work on the further revision of the New Testament. In the Uriya Scriptures, first translated by Dr. Carey and other Serampore missionaries, similar stages have to be recorded. To these the labours of the Church Missionary Society in Peshawar have added the Pashtu or Afghan Bible, completed in 1895. The New Testament and parts of the Old Testament were issued in Kashmiri from the Serampore press in 1820. In 1884 The Bible Society issued a revised New Testament prepared by the Rev. T. R. Wade (Church Missionary Society), and the whole Bible is now in course of publication.

Turning to South India, the main interest is concerned with the four great Bibles of the Dravidian languages.[1] The Tamil Bible, associated with the great names of Ziegenbalg, Fabricius, and Rhenius, after careful and prolonged revisions, was issued in its standard form in 1869. The Bible in Telugu—the Italian of the East—was ready in 1837, since which time it has been carefully and minutely revised. It owes much of its present form to the great Telugu scholar Dr. Hay (London Missionary Society). A revision committee, the end of whose labours appears still distant, has been at work upon it for the past twenty years. The Kanarese Bible, in print in 1832 through the persistent efforts of the Rev. John Hands (London Missionary Society), was revised by a united committee during another twenty years. At the present time a further committee is at work with the Rev. Henry Haigh (Wesleyan Missionary Society) as its chief reviser. The Malayalam New Testament was published in 1837 chiefly through the labours of the Rev. Benjamin Bailey

---

[1] These are Tamil, comprising 15 millions, Telugu 19 millions, Kanarese 9 millions, Malayalam 5 millions (*Expansion of Bible Society, 1837–1897*, p. 47).

(Church Missionary Society). Five years later the whole Bible was issued. Subsequent revision has been much delayed, in spite of the progress made in the lifetime of the Rev. C. Baker (Church Missionary Society); but the present committee, which has already completed the New Testament, happily appears to be making steady progress. Provision has been made for Ceylon in part by the Tamil Bible already mentioned, while the Sinhalese, who number 2,000,000, have a Bible with the New Testament satisfactorily revised, and the Old Testament in process of improvement.

The task of providing Christian literature for India is exceedingly vast and complex. As Sir William Hunter says in his lecture on the new forces in India, " We have thrown open the floodgates of a new moral and intellectual life in India, and the result is new energy, making itself felt in every department of human effort. The problems that have arisen are not merely political, but cover the whole area of Indian life and activity— moral, social, and religious." The task of the Church is to direct all this newly-awakened and awakening life into Christian channels, and books dealing with all questions from the Christian stand-point are essential. The number of readers in India is estimated at 20,000,000, with an annual increase of 2,000,000; but through the custom native readers have of gathering a circle of listeners around them, the written word may easily reach a much greater number. Three classes to be served may be enumerated. The first is composed of the 2,000,000 educated Hindus, "whose power and influence it is impossible to exaggerate",[1] and who are everywhere becoming the brain and voice of the country. They are in a state of religious restlessness, ready to admire the character and example of Jesus Christ, but

---

[1] *London Missionary Society Founders' Week Convention Report.* Paper by Rev. T. E. Slater, pp. 134–140.

for the most part unwilling to bear the offence of the cross, and from a mistaken patriotism endeavouring to revive and purify their Hinduism. Next, the vast masses must be considered who can only be reached through their vernaculars; and, finally, provision must be made for the education and instruction of the native Christian community. "Not only have the missionaries been the pioneers of vernacular education, they have also been among the first to employ the vernaculars as literary vehicles",[1] and the native press has of late wonderfully grown in power and influence. Out of the 7500 publications registered in India in 1893, at least 25 per cent were of a religious character, and the same description applies to a larger proportion of the 450 vernacular newspapers.[2] Unfortunately "reprints of the Puranas, with their discredited cosmogonies, stories of the deities and their incarnations and fabulous histories, the numerous erotic stories, some of which do so much to destroy the morals and corrupt the imagination of Hindu youth, are also being published and sold in large numbers all over the country",[3] and we must add that a constant stream of English agnostic and impure literature is pouring into the land. To meet these varied needs laborious efforts have been made by many missionaries, amongst whom Dr. Wilson of Bombay deserves special mention. No less than ten tract societies have been established in different parts of the Empire, whose work it is impossible to tabulate. Most conspicuous service has been rendered by the Christian Vernacular Education Society for India, which was founded in 1858 "as a memorial of the Lord's mercy

---

[1] *London Missionary Society Founders' Week Convention Report.* Paper by Rev. A. A. Dignum, p. 370.

[2] Among the useful vernacular periodicals the *Vrittanta Patrika*, in Canarese, published by the Wesleyan Missionary Society at Mysore, is doing great service.

[3] *London Missionary Society Founders' Week Convention Report*, pp. 370, 371.

in preserving India during the great Indian Mutiny ".
With two of the objects of this society—the training of
Christian native teachers, of whom in all 1173 have been
sent out from its institutions, and the establishment of
circles of schools, now numbering thirty-three—we are
not concerned here.   They have done and are doing
invaluable work; but the main object of the Christian
Literature Society for India, as it is now called, is to
provide text-books, manuals, and handbooks for educational purposes, and all kinds of literature for the
advancement of Christianity.   The list of publications
in various languages occupies 50 pages in the Report
for 1896, while the general figures from the commencement show that 2184 publications in eighteen languages
have been issued, making in all over 23,000,000 copies.
Dr. Murdoch's labours have been immense and varied
since he gave himself to this society in 1858, with the
hearty consent of the United Presbyterian Mission, to
which he belonged, and which has always contributed
liberally to his support.   Not only has he toiled for his
own society, but at the same time he has acted as
honorary superintendent of the various tract societies,
to which his advice and counsel have been of great
service and inspiration.   The books thus variously published touch all sides of life, comprising school-books,
general literature, papers on Indian reform, religious
reform, descriptions and examinations of Hindu sacred
books, &c., and tracts of various sizes.   Some provision has also been made of publications suitable for
women.   Among their writers must be named Mrs.
Mullens (London Missionary Society), whose story of
Phulmani and Karuna has been issued in several languages, and Miss Tucker of the Church Missionary
Society (better known under the initials A.L.O.E.),
whose many books and leaflets show how successfully
she attained her aim of "orientalizing her mind"; while

amongst native women writers, Mrs. Sattianadhan will not be forgotten. In all these undertakings little would have been achieved without the help of native translators and helpers. Among native authors we must mention Elias Gloria, Dr. Mohun Bannerjee, the Revs. Ram Chandra Bose, and Nehemiah Goreh Padmanji. Still much remains to be done, and the equipment of the native Church in commentaries and other aids to Bible study and theological works is sadly deficient. There are, however, encouraging indications that the great societies are becoming alive to the need, and the demand, specially emphasized at the Calcutta Conference in 1898, for the setting apart of suitable missionaries for literary work appears to be receiving more worthy attention.

The translation of the Scriptures into Persian dates from the version of the New Testament and Psalms achieved by the saintly Henry Martyn just before his death at Tokat in 1812, which remained unrevised for seventy years. In 1881 Dr. Bruce, assisted by the great linguist Professor Palmer, prepared a revision of the New Testament, to which a translation of the Old Testament has since been added. The New Testament and Psalms have also been published in the Arabic character, and the Pentateuch has been translated and printed in the Hebrew character. In a country presenting so many difficulties to mission work it is impossible to overestimate the importance of the printed book, especially when the people are so literary as the Persians. Many books and tracts are being issued from the Henry Martyn Memorial Press, established by the Church Missionary Society at Julfa. A Kurdish version of the New Testament is in course of preparation by the Rev. W. Tisdall (Church Missionary Society). A Persian edition of *Sweet First Fruits* is being lithographed by the Punjaub Tract Society, a method of production that saves trouble and delay in correcting proofs, and secures an exact reproduction of the Persian style of writing. *Sweet First Fruits* was written in Arabic by a native member of one of the Eastern Churches, who has renounced its ritual and practices and embraced the gospel in its simplicity. "The book is a romance, a delightful story, and as such well fitted to attract the oriental reader and rivet his attention. But its framework is primarily designed to give scope and opportunity for presenting to the Moslem reader the proofs of the Christian faith, the purity and genuineness of our Bible, its attestation by the Koran, and the consequent obligation on Moslems to obey its precepts."[1] Happily this book, which has also been published in Urdu, Pashtu, and other languages, is not alone, but forms one of many for Mohammedans, published in various languages, which have never yet been answered by those for whom their arguments and appeals are specially designed. Pfander, originally connected with the Basel Mission, but afterwards with the Church Missionary Society, and worthily described as the greatest of all missionaries to Mohammedans, wrote a most important and valuable book called *Mizan-al-Hagg* (Balance of Truth), which has been published in several languages. Another book deserving special mention is *The Beacon of Truth*, or the testimony of the Koran to the truth of the Christian religion, which has also been translated from the Arabic by Sir William Muir, and published by the Religious Tract Society. The needs of the 170,000,000 of Moslems, of whom 67,000,000 are to be found in India, are thus being met by the formation of a suitable literature in addition to the publication of the whole Bible in all the chief languages they speak, except the Hausa, which at present only has the New Testament and some parts of the Old.

[1] See English edition by Religious Tract Society, with preface by Sir William Muir, K.C.S.I.

Of the 40 Mission Bibles now in use in Asia, 17 were completed before 1837 ; 7 were begun before that year and have been completed since; and 16 are new. Of the 23 thus coming within our period, 9 are the work of non-British agencies. Of the 41 Asian New Testaments, 14 were completed before 1837; 3 were begun then and have been completed since; 24 are new, of which 4 are non-British. British agencies are thus to be credited with the addition (or completion) of 14 Bibles and 23 New Testaments for use in Asia.

In the great continent of Africa we find a vast mass of peoples almost entirely uncivilized and illiterate, amongst whom greater progress in Bible translation has been made than in any other part of the world. According to Dr. Cust there are six families of speech in Africa, viz. the Semitic, the Hamitic, the Nuba Fulah, the Negro, the Bantu, and the Hottentot, comprising 438 languages and 153 dialects, making 591 in all. By 1837 versions appear to have been made in 7 of these tongues; by 1897 no less than 98 are represented,[1] of which 14 have complete Bibles (omitting the Arabic, which has been reckoned in Asia). The only complete Bible in this part of the world in 1837 was the Malagasi, though the Amharic was then well-nigh finished. Of the other 12 which come strictly within our view, the Zulu alone is non-British, being the work of the American Bible Society. The Basuto version made by the Paris Missionary Society, and the Acra and Ashanti versions made by the Basel missionaries, must be reckoned as at least partly British, on account of the substantial help rendered by the British and Foreign Bible Society in printing and other ways, but as we are chiefly concerned here with British translations we shall give no further account of these.

The number of complete African New Testaments is

[1] Edmonds' *Expansion of Bible Society, 1837–1897*, p. 19.

now 19, omitting the Coptic. Of these only the ancient Ethiopic was in existence before 1837. Of the 18 new versions 4 only are non-British. British agencies have thus added during the sixty years 11 complete Bibles and 14 complete New Testaments to African literature.

The labour involved can hardly be overstated, as, with the exception of Arabic, it is tolerably correct to say that none of these languages had been previously written. The vast importance of the work is described in the following words of Dr. Cust: "As Luther's Bible became the standard of High German, and our own English Bible became the standard of later English, so all over Africa, from the language of the Kabail in North Africa to that of the Hottentot in the south, from the Swahili on the east to the Dualla on the west, the translation of the Book of Life is becoming the first, often the only, and always the typical, representative of languages which previously were wholly unwritten, uncultivated, and sometimes imagined to be destitute of phraseology for the expression of feelings and affections ".[1] The same authority declares that Africa will be indebted for advance in Christian civilization to the Roman character which is now employed in the African printing-presses and taught in the schools, though the Arabic character prevails in the north and has been carried to parts of the south by the Malay immigrants.

In South Africa we have first to mention the Kaffir Bible. Through the efforts of the Wesleyan missionaries, among whom the Rev. J. W. Appleyard deserves conspicuous praise, the Kaffir New Testament was issued in 1840 and the Old Testament about 1857. Subsequent revision has been repeatedly accomplished by a committee representing several societies. Various other literature has followed, including the *Pilgrim's Progress*

---

[1] Dr. Cust's *A Sketch of the Modern Languages of Africa*, vol. i. pp. 69, 70. Trubner & Co., 1883.

and the issue of an illustrated Kaffir Bible which is approaching completion.

The Sechuana Bible was the greatest achievement of Robert Moffat, whose fame is in all the churches. The Gospel of Luke was printed at Cape Town in 1830, and for ten years more, in the intervals of leisure, Moffat toiled at the remaining books, often, as he says, leaving the spade, the axe, or the anvil, to resume the pen. The New Testament and the Psalms were printed in England in 1840. The Old Testament was printed at Kuruman as the various books were ready, and the whole was completed in 1859. On his return home in 1871 Moffat revised the translation, but his improved text was never printed. A revised New Testament was issued in 1895, and the Old Testament is now undergoing careful revision. Other books have followed, the latest of which is a revised hymn-book with tunes. Further provision for Bechuanaland has been made in the Serolong New Testament, which was translated by Archdeacon Crisp (Society for the Propagation of the Gospel), and printed at the Thaba 'Nchu Mission Press. From the same press also have come several other beginnings of Christian literature.

In many other languages of South Africa progress is being made with Bible translation, though so far the New Testament alone has been attempted. Recent events demand the mention of the issue of St. Mark in Seshona (Wesleyan Missionary Society), and of the preparation of S. Luke for Matabeleland.

The complexity and difficulty of the task before the missionaries of Western Africa is exhibited in the monumental work of Dr. S. W. Koelle (Church Missionary Society), who about forty years ago published his *Polyglotta Africana*, in which vocabularies of some 200 languages were translated and compared.[1]

---

[1] Cust's *Modern Languages of Africa*, vol. i. p. 31.

In Sierra Leone, the first mission field of the Church Missionary Society, English is commonly spoken, but portions of Scripture have been prepared in three languages of neighbouring tribes. The Bible in Yoruba, spoken in Lagos and the neighbourhood, was completed in 1850, largely through the labours of Samuel Crowther, a native of the land, and afterwards the saintly Bishop of the Niger. The usual revision has followed here. In the Niger diocese portions have been issued in six languages, of which the most important is the Hausa, spoken far into the interior, even as far north as Tripoli. In this tongue there is already the New Testament, with the Psalms and Isaiah and some other portions of the Old Testament. A version is now being prepared in the Arabic character, but at present it only extends to some of the gospels. The provision of other Christian literature is following here as usual.

In the Efik, which is vernacular to the people living by the Old Calabar River, we find a complete Bible. The New Testament, translated by Rev. Hugh Goldie, of the United Presbyterian Mission, was published by the National Bible Society of Scotland in 1862. In 1868 the same society issued the Old Testament, translated by Rev. Dr. Alexander Robb of the same mission.

The Dualla is a widely-spoken language, being in use about the mouth of the Cameroons River, and extending in its many dialects across the equatorial region, where it finds close affinities with the tongues of the eastern coast. The New Testament was completed and printed by the Rev. Alfred Saker (Baptist Missionary Society) after immense labours from 1847 to 1862. Ten years later, on the completion of the Old Testament, he wrote: "The great work of years is now completed, and I feel as a bird long imprisoned, liberated at last, with permission to fly and enjoy the glories of an open sky. The victory is gained. The last sheet of the sacred volume, in good and readable type, is before me."[1] His later emendations found place in the edition of the New Testament published after his death in 1880.

To the same society belongs the place of honour in the Congo Mission, Stanley Pool being first reached by its representative in 1881. The Rev. W. H. Bentley has translated and printed the New Testament, with the assistance of Nlemo, his faithful native helper for eighteen years, and the beginnings of the Scriptures and of other Christian literature have been made in several languages.

In addition to the foregoing, versions of Scripture have been issued in some twenty other languages of Western Africa, amongst which may be mentioned the Temne New Testament (Church Missionary Society, 1867) and the Susu New Testament (Society for the Promotion of Christian Knowledge, 1883).

In East Africa conspicuous service was rendered by the Rev. Ludwig Krapf (Church Missionary Society), who at the beginning of our period revised the Amharic version of the Bible, and edited the New Testament in Amharic and Ethiopic, "so as to remove prejudice by exhibiting the living language side by side with the ancient version of the Ethiopic Church". Being driven out of Abyssinia by the intrigues of the French priests, he settled at Mombasa in 1844. In the following year he was joined by the Rev. John Rebmann (Church Missionary Society), with whom he gave himself to those "travels and geographical and linguistic studies which have, as a matter of fact, led directly to all the great Central African explorations of modern times".[2] Krapf compiled vocabularies in various languages, and a Swahili dictionary, into which tongue, with much help

---

[1] *The Centenary of the Baptist Missionary Society*, pp. 307, 308.

[2] *One Hundred Years, being the Short History of the Church Missionary Society*, p. 68, Eugene Stock.

from Rebmann, he translated nearly all the New Testament and a great part of the Prayer-book. He also published gospels in Nyika, Kamba, and Galla. In Galla, through the continued efforts of the Swedish Evangelical Missionary Society, the whole Bible has been completed, and is now being issued by The Bible Society. The great work in Swahili was accomplished by the Universities Mission, which, like the Tanganyika Mission of the London Missionary Society and the Livingstonia Mission of the Free Church of Scotland, owes its origin to the discoveries and inspiration of David Livingstone.[1] The Universities Mission has been favoured with a splendid succession of bishops,—Mackenzie, Tozer, Steere, Smythies, and Richardson,—amongst whom Steere is conspicuous for his translation work. Finding that Krapf had been misled into taking for his work a dialect of Swahili instead of the main language, Steere after five years' toil produced the Gospel of Matthew and a handbook in Swahili; in 1879 the New Testament was completed; and at his death he was found with the final proofs of Isaiah at his side. The whole Bible was finished in 1888 by Archdeacon Hodgson. Other devotional books and school primers have been provided. The *Pilgrim's Progress* in Chinyanja, with illustrations, is one of the latest additions.

In the Uganda Mission, which the Church Missionary Society began in 1876, remarkable progress has to be recorded. Alexander Mackay, a man of rare devotion and versatility, translated and printed at his native press a few chapters of S. Matthew. In carrying forward the work the Rev. R. P. Ashe gave great assistance, so that when Mr. G. L. Pilkington joined the mission in 1890 the Gospels of S. Matthew and

---

[1] Livingstone's parting words at Cambridge in 1857 deserve record here: " I go back to Africa to try to make an open path for commerce and Christianity. Do you carry out what I have begun. I leave it with you."

St. John had been published and the other gospels were translated. In a little more than twelve months Pilkington had published the first accurate Luganda handbook and vocabulary. By the middle of 1892 he had completed the New Testament and the Psalms. When the New Testament was published in 1893 the natives at once bought up all the copies. After revising the New Testament, with the help of the Rev. Henry Wright Duta, Pilkington completed the Old Testament, the whole of which was his work, except a few of the minor prophets. He also completed and revised the translation of the Prayer-book, and turned into Luganda, with additions, the first catechism of the Christian Vernacular Education Society of India, and composed a great number of favourite Luganda hymns. The whole Bible was issued in 1897,[1] and the *Pilgrim's Progress* has been published, so that provision has been made in large part for the Uganda readers, who are said to number 80,000.

In the Tanganyika Mission of the London Missionary Society the beginnings of a Christian literature have been made by the publication of vocabularies, hymnbooks, elementary lesson-books, the Gospel of S. Mark, and portions of S. Luke and S. John, in the Kimambwe tongue. At Urambo, which has recently been transferred to the Moravian Brethren, the Gospels of S. Matthew and S. Luke have been translated into Nyamwezi.

The Livingstonia Mission, established on Lake Nyassa in 1875 by the Free Church of Scotland, is carrying on important and extending work in twelve vernacular languages. The New Testament has been published in Nyanja, and S. Mark in Tonga. Laudable efforts also are being made to form one Bible version and one language for this region. The Nyanja dialect has been

---

[1] *Report of the Church Missionary Society*, 1898, pp. 122, 123.

selected, and if the attempt be successful it will prove a unifying force all over British Central Africa. The Mission Press at Livingstonia prints the mission's annual report in English, and has issued primers in Namwanga and Nyanja. The *Pilgrim's Progress* has been published in Tonga.

The Yao New Testament has just been printed, the translation having been prepared by the Rev. A. Hetherwick of the Church of Scotland Mission.[1]

The great African island of Madagascar, which has lately been made a French colony, has the most complete and advanced Christian literature in this part of the world. Before the fierce persecution of 1835 the Bible had been issued in Malagasi from the London Missionary Society's press in Antananarivo. The missionaries of that society had also published an idiomatic translation of the *Pilgrim's Progress*, some hymns, sermons, and tracts, all of which stood the bitterly persecuted Church in good stead for the next twenty-six years. When the mission was recommenced in 1862, attempts were at once made to provide efficient literature, and the success of the effort has been complete. All kinds of school-books, commentaries, dictionaries, sermons, medical works and monthly magazines have been published. In 1885 the Malagasi bibliography could only be given in twenty-nine octavo pages, and considerable additions have since been made. A complete revision of the Bible was issued in 1887, the work having been accomplished by a united committee, of which the Rev. W. E. Cousins (London Missionary Society) was the chief. To the London Missionary Society belongs the greater part of this work, but important help has been

---

[1] For an interesting summary of Bible translations in Africa, see *Africa Waiting*, by D. M. Thornton. Third edition, pp. 136, 137. Student Volunteer Missionary Union, London. Also Appendix C. on the *Work of all Bible Societies in Africa*, by Rev. J. Gordon Watt, M.A. *Ibid.*, pp. 146, 147.

given by the Friends, the Norwegians, and the Anglicans.[1] The circulation of 88,000 Bibles, of nearly a quarter of a million of New Testaments, and of 337,000 copies of single books of Scripture, affords solid ground for the belief that the Jesuits will fail in their attempt to overthrow the Protestantism of the Malagasi Churches.

For the scattered populations of the Pacific Islands beginnings had been made in 1837 by the Rev. Henry Nott (London Missionary Society), who was in England that year, with a complete Tahitian Bible, and by the Rev. John Williams (London Missionary Society), afterwards martyred at Erromanga, who had just brought home the Raratongan New Testament. There was also the Gospel of S. John in Samoan, the work of the same society. During the past sixty years these beginnings have grown to 11 complete Bibles (including the Maori), 11 New Testaments, and books or groups of books of Scripture in at least twenty-five other languages. Of these 11 Bibles the Tahitian alone was completed in 1837; 5 were begun before that year and have been completed since, and 5 are new; and of these 10 only 2 are non-British. All the 11 New Testaments have been produced since 1837; 4 of them are non-British. The record of British societies in this part of the world is accordingly 8 complete Bibles and 7 complete New Testaments.

The Tahitian Bible has passed through five editions, and has proved a bulwark to the natives in their resistance of the Roman Catholic propaganda. Hymn-books, elementary school-books, a few theological works, commentaries, the almost universal *Pilgrim's Progress*, and some simple periodicals complete the existing literature. Raratonga affords a similar list.   Its Bible, which was completed in 1850, has passed through four editions; its other literature is much the same as that of Tahiti. In Samoa, likewise, the Bible, completed in 1855, has

[1] Rev. G. Cousins, *Founders' Week Convention Report*, pp. 360, 361.

undergone careful revision by Pratt, Nisbet, Turner, and Murray—all of the London Missionary Society,—and was finished in 1872. With this admirable version of the Scriptures and his hymn-book the ordinary Samoan Christian appears contented. Other books (see pp. 121, 122) have been prepared for the schools and Malua Training Institution, and there is a fairly good equipment for Samoan pastors and missionaries to outlying islands.[1]

The Polynesian Bibles are completed by a reference to the Tonga version produced by the Wesleyan Missionary Society. The New Testament, begun in 1831, was issued in 1849 from the Mission Press at Vavau, and after another revision printed by The Bible Society. In 1860 The Bible Society also published the complete Bible. The Niué New Testament was begun by the Rev. W. G. Lawes and the Rev. George Pratt (London Missionary Society) in 1861; it was issued complete in 1867 by the New South Wales Auxiliary of The Bible Society. It has been subsequently revised, and a large part of the Old Testament has been added.

In Melanesia there are four complete Bibles to record. The New Testament was translated and printed in Fiji by Calvert, Hunt, and Lyth, of the Wesleyan Missionary Society, at the Fijian press in 1847. The second and third editions were printed by The Bible Society in 1854 and 1855. The Old Testament was translated by Hunt and Hazelwood (Wesleyan Missionary Society), and published by The Bible Society in 1864. The usual revision has followed, and is now being again completed by the Rev. F. Langham (Wesleyan Missionary Society). In the other Fijian literature, which is not of an advanced character, the *Pilgrim's Progress* appears.

In the New Hebrides the Aneityum Bible was prepared by the Presbyterian missionaries Revs. John Geddie and John Inglis, who came from Nova Scotia and New

[1] Rev. G. Cousins, *Founders' Week Convention Report*, pp. 357, 358.

Zealand. Through their labours the New Testament was published in 1863, and the complete Bible in 1878. Here also we may mention the Tanna New Testament, of which S. Mark—translated by the Rev. J. G. Paton of New Hebrides fame—was printed in 1862. The remainder of the Testament was prepared by the Rev. W. Watt of the same mission, and issued complete in 1890 by the National Bible Society of Scotland. In the New Hebrides there is also the Faté New Testament, begun in 1864 by the Rev. D. Morrison, a Presbyterian of Nova Scotia. It was completed in 1888 and published by The Bible Society.

The Maré New Testament was prepared and printed in the island by the Rev. J. Jones (London Missionary Society) in 1867. It has since been revised and issued with parts of the Old Testament by The Bible Society.

The two remaining Bibles are the Lifuan and the Uvean, both of the Loyalty Islands. As early as 1855 the first chapter of S. John's Gospel in Lifuan was prepared by the Rev. William Nihill (Society for the Propagation of the Gospel) and printed in Maré. The first gospel published was S. Mark, which was translated by Bishop Patteson and printed in New Zealand in 1859. In the same year the Rev. Samuel M'Farlane (London Missionary Society) issued S. Matthew's Gospel from the Maré press. The New Testament was completed in 1868, and has passed through three editions. The complete Bible was ready in 1884, and was issued after revision in 1888.

For Uvea the Psalms and New Testament were ready in 1869. The Rev. John Hadfield (London Missionary Society) has revised and completed the work, and is now seeing through the press the first edition of the whole Bible.

The Rev. John Coleridge Patteson, who joined the Melanesian Mission in 1854 and succeeded Bishop

Selwyn as Bishop of Melanesia in 1861, reduced twenty-three Melanesian languages to writing, and compiled and issued elementary grammars of thirteen tongues, and shorter abstracts of eleven others. Most of these, with translations of the British Prayer-book and portions of the New Testament, were printed by native pupils of the Melanesian College at Kohimarama, New Zealand, between 1863 and 1868.[1]

The Mota New Testament (Banks Islands) was issued by the Society for the Promotion of Christian Knowledge in 1884, and the Rotuma New Testament (prepared by the Rev. W. Fletcher of the Wesleyan Society) was issued by The Bible Society (Sydney) in 1870. In 1884 it was revised and seen through the same press by the Rev. James Calvert (Wesleyan Missionary Society).

The remaining complete Bible[2] in this part of the world is the version prepared for the Maoris of New Zealand, who are said to number 40,000. The New Testament was completed in 1837 by the Rev. W. Williams (Church Missionary Society). In 1859 the whole Bible was issued as translated by Rev. R. Maunsell (Church Missionary Society). Revision has been made with the help of the Wesleyan missionaries, and two editions issued. The latest publication is a revised Psalter and New Testament under the direction of Bishop Williams of Waiapu.

Torres Strait and New Guinea present a perfect babel of languages. Translations of some parts of Scripture have been so far made into eleven tongues, of which the chief are the Murray Island Gospels of S. Mark and S. John made by the Revs. S. M'Farlane and H. Scott (London Missionary Society); the Saibai S. Matthew

---

[1] *Digest of Society for the Propagation of the Gospel Records, 1701-1892,* p. 805.

[2] The reckoning excludes the Gilbert and the Hawaiian Bibles, which are of American origin.

and S. Mark revised by the Rev. S. M'Farlane in 1883; the Motuan New Testament and parts of the Old Testament issued by Dr. Lawes and the Rev. J. Sunderland (London Missionary Society) in 1884; the Keapara Gospels, Acts, and parts of the Old Testament now being revised by the Rev. A. Pearse (London Missionary Society), and printed by The Bible Society. The remaining six tongues have at present only one gospel, which in five cases is that of S. Mark. There are also three hymn-books and other slight beginnings of literature.

In the great continent of America complete Bibles have been produced in four languages spoken by the North-American Indians. Of these, the Eskimo, translated by the Moravians between 1810 and 1870, was issued by The Bible Society in 1871; the Dakota, published in 1879, is the work of the American Bible Society. In the Cree Eastern dialect the Bible was prepared in the syllabic character by the Rev. W. Mason (Church Missionary Society) between 1854 and 1861; and the New Testament by Bishop Horden was published in the Roman character in 1876. In Tudukh the four Gospels were completed in 1874, and a revised New Testament in 1885 through the efforts of the Church Missionary Society, while the whole Bible has now passed through the press of The Bible Society. There are also 8 New Testaments in other North-American languages, of which 2 were completed before 1837, 3 are non-British, and 3 are the work of British Church missions; so that the record of British societies in America is 3 complete Bibles and 3 New Testaments. There are, in addition, in about twenty tongues, hymns, prayers, and other elementary beginnings of Christian literature.

Four of the Indian languages of British Guiana were reduced to writing by the Rev. W. H. Brett of the Society for the Propagation of the Gospel. In two of

these—the Arawak and the Acawoio—portions of the
New Testament have been published by the Society for
the Promotion of Christian Knowledge, in addition to
Prayers and Catechisms.   Smaller efforts have been
made in Carib and Warau.

The South American Mission, which is the outcome of
the Patagonian Mission founded by the heroic Captain
Gardiner in 1844, has reduced the Yahgan and Quichua
Indian languages to writing.   By the labours of the
Rev. Thomas Bridges of that mission, S. Luke, S. John,
and the Acts are available for the Yahgan-speak-
ing people of Tierra del Fuego.   The Rev. Gybbon
Spilsbury has provided S. John for the Quichua Indians
of the interior of the Argentine Republic.

This brief and necessarily imperfect sketch may be
sufficient to show the important part that the production
of Christian literature plays in the various fields.   All
societies have had their share in it, though some have
been able to do more than others.   The starting of a
new mission at once involves translation work, for without an elementary literature, at least, no equipment can
be regarded as at all sufficient.   Old and well-established
missions are perpetually confronted by the need of
revising and increasing their productions.   The progress
of the last sixty years in these directions has been truly
marvellous.   Efforts have been made to recognize, if not
to meet, the demands of all countries and classes.   Even
the unfortunate blind thousands of many lands have been
remembered, and books in the Braille system have been
issued for their benefit in China, India, Japan, and Africa.
At the same time we have only been able for the most
part to report beginnings.   As the work advances, and
the native churches grow in numbers and intelligence, a
native Christian literature will spring up more thoroughly
adapted to local needs than the products of foreign missionaries.   In the meantime, while thankful for what has

been accomplished, we would earnestly call the attention of all friends of missions to the growing importance of this department of labour, and to the serious gaps that still exist in China and India, not to mention other lands. From all the fields there comes a loud call for a closer grappling with the task of meeting the various needs of the unenlightened millions of mankind, and of recognizing as an essential part of the missionary staff the literary missionary whose time and energy may be fully consecrated to this service.

In closing this chapter we may summarize the means adopted for the distribution and circulation of such literature as exists. In the hundreds of stations scattered throughout the world, by the workers who are happily counted to-day by tens of thousands, and by innumerable native Christians, Christian books are being read and scattered abroad. In addition to these, the Bible Society is pouring forth a saving literature from 100 depots in heathen lands and through the 455 colporteurs and 504 Bible-women that it supports in non-Christian countries. The Religious Tract Society, with its many branches, is engaged in the same work, while the National Bible Society for Scotland maintains 281 colporteurs among the heathen. If we look at the growth, or rather the multiplication, of all these agencies during the past sixty years, we shall find much cause for encouragement; but if we try to imagine the vast fields "already white unto the harvest", the encouragement of the past should only lead us to see that more labourers are sent forth, and that adequate equipment is provided for their gigantic task.

Chapter VI.

Special Developments—Medical Missions.

There are many grounds on which medical missions must be regarded as an essential and integral part of the foreign missionary enterprise. The first to be mentioned here is the obvious duty of showing that Christianity has salvation for the body as well as for the soul, and is designed to renew and vitalize all parts of man's activity.[1] In view of the immense suffering of heathen people, and their almost complete ignorance of medicine and surgery, it would seem to be the divine will that the healing of the sick and the proclamation of the kingdom of Heaven should still be closely associated. "I take it", says Dr. Fox,[2] "that the true work of the medical profession is but a particular case of the whole gamut of philanthropic effort made for the temporal good of mankind, such as feeding, housing, and clothing the hungry and destitute, liberating the slave, reconciling enemies, raising the fallen through vice or intemperance, tending the weak, teaching the ignorant, and guiding the erring into the paths of righteousness, industry, and peace. All these owe their origin to, or still draw their chief support from, Christianity; and most of them can be suitably brought into the service of foreign missions. The Medical Mission is an attempt to retain an intimate connection between the work for the body and for the soul, and is therefore strictly comparable to the other branches of mission work, such as the educational, the industrial, &c."

The prevalent heathen idea that sickness and suffering

---

[1] See *Christian Missions and Social Progress*, vol. i. *passim*, J. S. Dennis, D.D. Oliphant, Anderson, & Ferrier.

[2] *Friends' Foreign Missions, Darlington Conference*, 1896. London: West, Newman, & Co. 1897.

in their varied forms result from the persons affected being possessed by evil spirits would of itself demand the efforts of the medical missionary; while the cruel and barbarous treatment of the sick that follows from such a theory may well stir to activity the compassion of any who have experienced the healing or assuaging powers of western medical science. "The sick person", says Mrs. Isabella Bishop, "becomes an object of loathing and terror, is put out of the house, is taken to an outhouse, is poorly fed and rarely visited; or, the astrologers or priests, or medicine-men, or wizards assemble, beating big drums and gongs, blowing horns, and making the most fearful noises. They light gigantic fires, and dance round them with their unholy incantations. They beat the sick person with clubs to drive out the demon. They lay him before a roasting fire till his skin is blistered, and then throw him into cold water. They stuff the nostrils of the dying with aromatic mixtures or mud, and in some regions they carry the chronic sufferer to a mountain top, placing barley-balls and water beside him, and leave him to die alone."[1] To this general description may be added a particular case described by Dr. Greig of the Irish Presbyterian Mission, after reaching Kirin in Manchuria:—

"The day after we arrived, when sitting in our room waiting for our way to open up, we were startled by dreadful screams coming from the other side of the yard of the inn. We made enquiries, and found that a native doctor and sorcerer was treating the daughter-in-law of the innkeeper for being 'possessed of a devil', and that he had succeeded in getting the evil spirit up into her arms and would soon get it out.

"We refrained from interfering for a short time, but

[1] Speech in Exeter Hall, November 1893. Published by the Church Missionary Society.

as the screaming continued and betokened great suffering, we went across to see if we could not render
some assistance. The sight which met our gaze was
ghastly. In a small room, crowded with men and
women, the sorcerer was carrying on his diabolical
work. His patient—a poor woman of thirty years of
age—was held down by a number of strong men upon
the kang, or bed, and was simply writhing in agony.
Two large needles were sticking through her upper lip,
and others were being forced up under her finger nails.
Some of the largest veins in the forearm had just been
opened, and the dark venous blood was pouring out.
The ignorant and superstitious people, pointing to the
blood, cried, ' Look at its colour; it is well to let it
out '. The colour was really that of healthy venous
blood. It was in vain that we protested against this
inhuman cruelty. Warnings and pleadings were alike
fruitless, and the exorcist proceeded, looking a little
angry, however, at our expostulations. Incense sticks
were shortly produced and burned before him whilst he
muttered some prayers and went through a series of
fanatical gesticulations, such as gulping down the devil,
and slapping himself on his forehead, &c. After he
left, the story we got from the mother-in-law of the
patient seemed to indicate that the subject of these
tortures was suffering from some infectious fever, and
had for some nights been delirious. This the poor people
thought was ' possession by a devil '. Next morning,
to our horror, we learned that the woman had died
during the night." [1]

From many peculiar prescriptions that might be mentioned, we may give the following : " Tiger's bones are
given to the weak and debilitated as a strengthening medicine, and those who cannot afford such an expensive luxury

---

[1] Quoted in *The Edinburgh Medical Missionary Society* by Dr. Sargood
Fry.

may yet obtain some of the strength and courage of that ferocious beast by swallowing a decoction of the hairs of his moustache, which are retailed at the low price of 100 cash apiece ".[1]

The complete absence of any effective practice of surgery or medicine among the Chinese may be inferred from the fact that they had no acquaintance with anatomy or physiology till it was brought into the country by medical missionaries.[2] The condition of things here indicated presses with peculiar hardness upon women in heathen lands, for they necessarily suffer more than men from the prevailing ignorance of the laws of health and from the absence of proper treatment in times of need and sickness. No relief can be brought to the secluded women of India and China save by some of their own sex, for when a medical man has been called as a last resource to a Zenana or harem, he is expected to prescribe not only without examining the patient, but even without seeing her. He may be allowed to see her tongue or to feel her pulse through a hole in the curtain! The high death-rate among women and children in India has more than justified the medical aid rendered by the Government and the establishment of the Lady Dufferin Fund; but the highest work can only be accomplished by the medical missionary, and among women the fully-qualified medical woman alone can render the needed service.[3]

[1] Rev. A. W. Douthwaite, M.D.: *Record of Missionary Conference at Shanghai, 1890.* American Press, Shanghai, p. 290.

[2] For illustrations of this in China and other lands, see Lowe, *Medical Missions* (London: Fisher Unwin), chapter vi.

[3] In this connection the following extract from a Buddhist writing is suggestive: No physician is worthy of waiting on the sick unless he has five qualifications for his office. 1. The skill to prescribe the proper remedy. 2. The judgment to order the proper diet. 3. The motive must be life and not greed. 4. He must be content and willing to do the most repulsive office for the sake of those whom he is waiting upon. 5. *He must be both able and willing to teach, to incite, and to gladden the hearts of those whom he is attending, by religious discourse.* Quoted in *Encyclopædia of Missions,*

It is necessary also to make provision for the needs of converts from heathenism. If they become ill they are naturally and strongly urged by their heathen friends to seek the only relief known to them, through the medicine-man. Cases are numerous in which sickness has led to a relapse into the former darkness and superstition.

In many parts of the field the health, and sometimes the life, of the missionary staff is dependent upon the presence of a missionary doctor, so that it is not surprising that some maintain that no missionary station is properly manned without such helpers. This may not be the case everywhere, for in many centres in India and China a general practitioner is available, but there are many large districts still where no such aid is at hand. In all Congo land, for example, with an estimated population of nearly 50,000,000, there are but two hospitals and no more than ten qualified physicians—whether on the Government or missionary staff. How urgent the need must be at times is clear from the distance between the stations, which varies from 20 to 200 miles.[1]

A still stronger reason for medical missions, if one be required, is found in their immense service as a pioneer agency. They have succeeded in gaining entrance for the gospel message when other means have failed. Meeting the lower and—for the time—the more clamorous need, they have opened closed doors and effectually revealed the loving and helpful aim with which missionaries have gone into heathen lands. Sufferers and their friends are quickly touched by acts of kindness and deeds of healing done to those who previously regarded their presence with grave suspicion and credited

vol. ii. p. 49, Art. "Medical Missions", edited by Rev. E. M. Bliss. New York and London: Funk & Wagnalls. 1891.

[1] Rev. H. D. Campbell, *Student Missionary Appeal*, *S.V.M.U.*, pp. 490, 491. New York, 1898.

them with doubtful motives. The presentation of Christianity in such a concrete form is readily appreciated. Out of many illustrations two may be mentioned here. The Church Missionary Society attempted to enter Kashmir as early as 1854, but was obliged to withdraw through violent opposition, and made no further attempt till 1862. The missionaries sent in that year were also unsuccessful. In 1865 a medical mission, under Dr. Elmslie, proved the means of effectually opening the country for Christian work. In 1879 successful service was rendered in Tientsin by Dr. Mackenzie (London Missionary Society), in conjunction with two other physicians, to Lady Li, wife of His Excellency Li Hung Chang. As an expression of gratitude, facilities were given for the establishment of a medical mission in that city, and—though, through some misunderstanding, official help was afterwards withdrawn—it may be said that the first genuine Chinese medical school was a direct result of Dr. Mackenzie's influence; while several of its first teachers were Christian Chinese who had received from him their medical training.

The history of British medical missions falls almost entirely within our period, though some valuable preliminary work had been attempted prior to 1837. Mr. Thomas, who had been in India as a surgeon of the East India Company, went out with Carey in 1793, and was associated for many years with the Serampore mission. The Society for the Propagation of the Gospel also from early times in its history has had medically-qualified men upon its staff. It is interesting to observe that a surgeon was among the first party sent out by the London Missionary Society on the *Duff* in 1796, and that under the same society Robert Morrison, the first Protestant missionary to China,— with the help of Dr. Livingstone, a surgeon of the East India Company, — dispensed medicines to sick

Chinamen at Macao as early as 1820. Seven years later Dr. Colledge, who succeeded Dr. Livingstone, opened and sustained a dispensary at his own charges, and in the first four years ministered to 4000 patients. Meanwhile the American Congregational Board had given more definite recognition to this form of service by sending Dr. Scudder in 1819 to Ceylon. Dr. Scudder afterwards went to India, and spent in all thirty-six years as a medical missionary. In 1834 the same society began similar work in Canton by the appointment of the Rev. Peter Parker, M.D., who is said to have opened China to the gospel at the point of the lancet, and whose visit to England in 1841 led to the formation of the Edinburgh Medical Missionary Society.

The first regular British medical missionary was Dr. Kalley, who went out at his own cost to Madeira in 1837, and accomplished work there which at the time was spoken of as "the greatest fact in modern missions". Later on he went to Malta, Syria, and South America, where he accomplished equally successful labours.[1] In 1838 Mr. A. Ramsay, a surgeon, was sent by the London Missionary Society to Travancore, and laid the foundations of that society's present large medical work in Neyoor. A year later Dr. Lockhart, also of the London Missionary Society, took charge of the hospital which Dr. Parker had established at Macao; and British missions of this kind were fairly begun as a recognized part of the missionary enterprise. In 1839 Dr. Hobson (London Missionary Society) arrived at Macao, and carried on work there till 1843, when he established a hospital at Hong Kong. In addition to service at Hong Kong and Canton, Dr. Hobson materially promoted the advance of medical science in China by the publication of treatises in Chinese on anatomy, surgery, medicine, midwifery and natural

[1] Lowe's *Medical Missions*, pp. 139-143.

philosophy, many of which have also been widely circulated in Japan.

Considerable advance was made in 1841 by the formation of the Edinburgh Association for sending Medical Aid to Foreign Countries, which two years later assumed its well-known title of the Edinburgh Medical Missionary Society. The impulse which led to this came from the earnest representations of the Rev. Peter Parker, M.D., already mentioned, who, visiting Edinburgh on his way to China from America, secured the interest of Dr. Abercrombie in medical mission work. Dr. Abercrombie called the meeting out of which the society sprang, and became its first president. For the first few years the funds collected were mainly expended in diffusing knowledge about such missions, and in grants for the purchase of medicines and instruments to the few medical missionaries then in the field. The next step was to give financial help to students who were preparing for the service. In 1853 this was followed by the establishment, under Dr. Handyside, of the Main Point Dispensary, which was the first *Home* Medical Mission and the origin of the society's training institution. The society now provides its students of both sexes—who are drawn from various denominations both at home and abroad — with a full medical and surgical education at the University, or Extra Mural School of Medicine, along with a thorough practical training in the various departments of missionary work. Its equipment for its important work was completed by the erection of its present home, the Livingstone Memorial Medical Missionary Training Institute, at a cost of £10,000. The first student was Dr. Paterson, who for more than ten years was the society's agent in Madras. Amongst many deserving mention we must not pass over the name of Dr. Wong Fan of Canton, who, under this society's auspices, was the first Chinese graduate of a

European university, and who was for many years the colleague of Dr. Hobson previously mentioned. At the end of 1897 no less than 78 men and women who had been trained within its walls were actively engaged in medical mission work, 72, of whom 3 were women, being in the foreign field. In addition to the invaluable work of training missionaries at home, the society engages in direct mission work abroad. It has maintained for many years an important training institution at Agra, under one of its own students, the Rev. Dr. Valentine, and, since 1861 and 1884, similar institutions at Nazareth and Damascus.

Since the formation of the Edinburgh Medical Missionary Society, and in many cases through its influence and assistance, medical mission work has gained increasing recognition. In 1841 there were only 4 medical missionaries in the field, and the London Missionary Society alone among British societies had definitely engaged in that kind of service; at the end of 1897 there were 197 men and 54 women holding British diplomas in the service of 39 British societies, making a total of 251.[1] The Church Missionary Society, which began this work by sending Dr. Elmslie to Kashmir in 1865, employs 44 of these; the Free Church of Scotland has 29; the London Missionary Society, 24; the United Presbyterian Church, 21; while 8 belong to the Society for the Propagation of the Gospel, and the remainder in smaller numbers to other agencies. Out of the total of 251, 87 are at work in India and 85 in China; 38 in Africa; 12 in Palestine; 6 in Turkey; 5 in the South Seas; 4 in Syria; 3 in Madagascar; 3 in Persia; 2 in Korea; 1 in Japan; 1 in Java; 1 in North-west America; and 3 in fields not coming within our view.

---

[1] See list given in *Medical Missions at Home and Abroad*, January, 1898. To these must be added a few medical missionaries with other than British qualifications.

The Medical Missionary Association of London was established in 1878 with the three objects of assisting young men in the training necessary for medical mission work abroad, of encouraging and assisting in the planting of medical missions at home and abroad, and of promoting medical mission interest among the students of our medical schools as well as throughout the profession and among the Christian public.   About 12 of its former students are now in the foreign field connected with different societies, and 16 are still pursuing their studies.   The association publishes a valuable monthly magazine called *Medical Missions at Home and Abroad*, from which some quotations are made in this chapter.

In addition to the fully-qualified medical missionaries mentioned above, a large number of men—at work chiefly in the less-civilized fields—have acquired, before going out, some knowledge of elementary medicine and surgery which enables them, in the absence of qualified help, to preserve their own health and to render service to those among whom they labour; but they are not to be reckoned as medical missionaries.   The Livingstone College—established in London in 1893 under the presidency of Dr. Harford-Battersby, formerly a missionary of the Church Missionary Society on the Niger—provides a two years' course which is laid out for such training, and has helped in the preparation of 70 men connected with various societies; but it marks the distinction between its students and regular medical missionaries.   Many women missionaries have also undergone in other institutions a somewhat similar training, or have qualified in nursing and midwifery; but none of these can be reckoned as medical missionaries, though they perform much good work in connection with hospitals and dispensaries, in teaching hygiene to native women, and in assisting them in their times of need.

The nature and extent of medical mission work may be indicated under the divisions of the dispensary and hospital, home visitation, itinerating, and the medical school. In every branch the object is not only to heal the sick, but to use all opportunities afforded to make the gospel known. The work is usually begun by the establishment of a dispensary, in which a short service is held before the patients are examined by the doctor; and while they are waiting their turn, other Christian workers are able to go in and out among them. Before long, in-patients have to be received, and then, if funds permit, the hospital is built. To all in-patients, except those seriously ill, systematic Christian instruction is given. Many are influenced by the gospel message, and go forth healed in soul as well as in body, and carry to their homes— often many miles distant—the seeds of Christian truth, or at least a favourable report of the foreigners' kindness and skill. As a typical illustration, reference may be made to the Swatow Medical Mission, which was begun in 1862 by Dr. Gauld of the English Presbyterian Church, in a Chinese house fitted up to accommodate a few in-patients. Since then it has grown to be the largest medical mission in China, and "drew its patients in 1896 from no fewer than 1221 towns and villages in the regions around. Of nearly 3000 in-patients received during the year, the average time of residence in the hospital was *three weeks*. During that period each patient was in *daily contact* with *Christian teaching* and *Christian practice*. Out of 100 applicants 18 were received by baptism into the Church. For the support of the hospital no more than £100 was required from this country."[1] A few years ago the Rev. W. Macgregor of the Amoy Mission of the same Church told of a man who, seventeen years before, came

<hr />

[1] *China and Formosa*, by Rev. James Johnston, p. 285. London: Hazell, Watson, & Viney. 1898.

from an unevangelized district of the country to the hospital at Amoy, where he was successfully treated. On his return home he so effectually delivered the message of the gospel that a number believed. After a teacher had been sent by the missionaries at their request, a congregation of about 100 was gathered. Many came from a considerable distance, and a new community had to be formed inland. The work went on increasing till seven congregations—each numbering from 30 to upwards of 100 persons—were formed as the result of the good seed sown in that one patient's heart while in the mission hospital.[1] Similar records might be given, did space permit, from nearly all other medical centres.

Another important effect of the dispensaries is the bringing together of different castes and peoples, as, for instance, in North India, the Hindu and Mohammedan, Brahmin and Sudra, Jew and native Christian, Eurasian, Parsee, and European. In some dispensaries the admission is by ticket, on which is also written a verse of Scripture. If the poorest outcast gets the first ticket of admission, she is the first attended to.

No small amount of work is done amongst patients in their homes. The opportunities of regular Christian instruction are not great, but there are many sufferers, whom custom would not allow to visit a dispensary or hospital, reached in this way, especially by lady medical missionaries. The following record of a day's engagements given by a missionary doctor that his friends at home might better imagine his life, is of interest as showing the varied and full occupation in which such workers are engaged:—

" 1. Rode out to see a wealthy merchant who was ill. 2. Paid a visit to the widow of a missionary who was seriously ill. 3. Worked up the estimates and

[1] From Lowe's *Medical Missions*, pp. 132, 133.

list of medicines required from England, and wrote letters. 4. Breakfasted. 5. Did more correspondence. 6. Visited a European lady who was ill. 7. Took service at the church and gave an address on Barnabas, his life and work; being S. Barnabas' Day. 8. Gave an address in the vernacular to the out-patients. 9. Saw out-patients. 10. Saw one or two European cases who had come for consultation. 11. Had an interview with a Mohammedan who had been interfering with the building work, and succeeded in pacifying him. 12. Visited the building work. 13. Went all round the hospital wards. 14. Gave a second address to out-patients. 15. Saw second batch of out-patients. 16. Went to the leper hospital to see patients and do a little office work. 17. Went back to the hospital for afternoon rounds. 18. Saw two private patients, one two miles away. 19. Paid a second visit to the missionary's widow. 20. Dined. 21. Visited another private case. 22. In response to an urgent summons about 10 P.M., went down the river to see someone who was very ill." [1]

The mention of a leper hospital in the foregoing extract naturally suggests a brief reference to the important and growing efforts to alleviate the sufferings of that most afflicted class. It is said that there are nearly half a million lepers in India alone, while large numbers are to be found in other eastern lands, and even Madagascar is not without them. One of the first leper asylums in India was established at Almora, in 1849, by the Rev. J. H. Budden (London Missionary Society). Since that time similar institutions have been so multiplied that they are now found in fifty-two stations in India, Burmah, Ceylon, China, Japan, and Madagascar. Much of this advance is due to the devoted efforts of Mr. Wellesley C. Bailey,

[1] *Mercy and Truth: A Record of C.M.S. Medical Mission Work,* January, 1899.

who joined the American Presbyterian Mission in the Punjaub in 1869, and spent twelve years in India, during all of which he was interested in work among lepers, and for part of which he was in charge of two leper asylums. During his visit to Ireland in 1874 a sum of £30 annually was promised for the relief of such sufferers, and the Mission to Lepers in India was established. In 1893 the title was enlarged, and the society became The Mission to Lepers in India and the East. In 1897, in addition to helping nine British and several other missionary societies, the mission had twenty hospitals of its own, and a number of homes for the untainted children of lepers, and expended £7592 in its work. The number of inmates in the mission's homes is about 1000, while those in aided institutions mount up to 1700. In all cases Christian instruction is given as well as treatment and shelter, and no form of Christian effort is more rich in spiritual results or more quick in its effects. The proportion of those brought into asylums who become Christians is very large, and the indirect influence on the surrounding heathen is considerable, for such work is an object-lesson which they cannot explain away.[1]

The itinerating work shall be described in his own words by Dr. Campbell (London Missionary Society) of Jammulamadugu, South India. Writing in 1892, he says: "We live in tents about half the year, so that we may be able to visit the numerous villages. Having travelled by train or country bullock-cart to some village, we pitch our tents and make it a centre of work for several days, visiting all the villages and hamlets within a radius of three or four miles. Then we pass on to another village, and so for about twenty days we go from place to place preaching in all the villages by the

---

[1] See *A Visit to Leper Asylums in India and Burma, 1895-6*, by Wellesley C. Bailey. Edinburgh: Hunter.

way. When in camp we rise at dawn, and after a hurried cup of tea start off for the village, that we may get an audience before the people go to their work in the fields or at the loom. When we get to the village we take our stand in the central street, generally in front of a little rudely-made village temple, and soon gather an audience of men, women, and children by singing one of our Telugu Christian lyrics. The people squat round us on the ground, and listen attentively while we tell them the good news of the gospel. We try to make our address very simple and practical. We do not, as a rule, attack their religious systems, but try, by presenting the Lord Jesus Christ to them, to let them see the emptiness of their own religious beliefs. . . . During one tour of eighteen days we visited and preached in about seventy villages, and in almost all of these the people heard us gladly. Often they say to us, 'Why do you not come oftener and tell us this good news? We wish to hear more.' Very often it is twelve or one o'clock before we get back from the villages for breakfast. Sometimes I have as many as 100 patients to see in the afternoon, and very often darkness comes on before I have seen them all."

Such an account recalls the first and greatest medical missionary Who "went about all the cities and the villages . . . preaching the Gospel of the Kingdom, and healing all manner of diseases and all manner of sickness ".

Two or three instances may be given of the training of Christian native students to become medical evangelists to their countrymen. The largest establishment for this purpose is the Medical Missionary Training Institution in Agra, where the Government Medical College is utilized for the medical classes. The Principal of the Institution is the Rev. Colin S. Valentine, LL.D., F.R.S.C.E., who began his successful career

in connection with the United Presbyterian Mission in
1861. It was through his influence that the native
state of Jeypore was opened to Christianity. The Agra
Institution was opened in 1884 and affiliated with the
Edinburgh Medical Missionary Society in 1885, by
which it has since been supported. "Christian Indian
students of both sexes, chosen by the different missionaries of North India independently of any one de-
nomination, are received into the Institution, attend the
four years' curriculum of medicine in the Government
College and religious and other instruction from Dr.
Valentine and his assistant. They then become most
valuable assistants to medical missionaries, and, in
some cases, take independent charge of mission dispensaries or hospitals. In this way between twenty and
thirty stations are already occupied by former students
of the Institution, and there are ten or twelve students
now in training. £10 per annum (£40 in all) will
provide a complete scholarship for one of these young
men."

Similar work is being accomplished in many other
medical missions, in fact the natural progress is from
the dispensary to the hospital, and where funds and
staff are sufficient, to the medical school. For many
years in Travancore, under Dr. Lowe and Dr. Fry
(who afterwards in succession became superintendents
of the Edinburgh Medical Missionary Society) and
others, the London Missionary Society has effectively
conducted all parts of medical mission work, having
at the present time six hospitals and ten dispensaries, which are managed by 1 European doctor and
a missionary nurse, helped by 20 native assistants.
Itinerating work also is accomplished. In Hong Kong
the local European practitioners have instituted a
Chinese Medical School. For the training of their
students they make use of the two mission hospitals

conducted by the same society. It is interesting to record that the larger of these hospitals, in which the local doctors render valuable and gratuitous service, was built at the expense of a Chinese gentleman.

Till quite recently there has been no provision made for the training of native Christian women even in India as fully-qualified medical missionaries. The Indian Government has made it possible for native women to qualify in the Government medical schools, but the Government arrangements do not meet the needs of the missionary societies. Their schools are of necessity non-religious, and any attempt to provide for the religious instruction and oversight of any Christian women during their course at such schools was resented by the authorities, and it was found in consequence that such pupils were likely to relapse into heathenism. Besides this, strong objection has been raised by the natives themselves to the instruction in these schools being given to mixed classes of men and women by male lecturers. In 1894, to avoid these difficulties, the North Indian School of Medicine for Christian Women was founded at Ludhiana. Its objects are to supply qualified Christian native assistants to aid in the various medical missions for women, and to provide a five years' course for the diploma of Licentiate in Medicine and Surgery. The staff, which is completed in the various branches, consists of fully-qualified Christian medical women. On the committee of management are representatives of eight missionary societies, three of which are American and five are British. Hospital practice is obtained at the Charlotte Hospital of the Society for Promoting Female Education in the East, where nearly 1200 operations were performed last year, and at the Memorial Hospital belonging to the school. Regular Bible instruction is given to the students, and every care is taken to qualify them spiritually as well as medically. The number of students is now 26. The Government has recognized the value of this school by sanctioning the admission of its students who wish for Government qualification to the examination given by the Lahore Medical College for hospital assistants. There can be no doubt that there is a future of great usefulness amongst Indian women in store for this admirably-planned and much-needed institution.

We cannot conclude this chapter without giving some general figures of the British medical profession, and asking if a fair proportion of those who hold British diplomas are devoting themselves to this important service. In 1898 there were 28,589 doctors in Great Britain and Ireland holding British degrees or diplomas, and in addition to these 3770 with similar qualifications practising abroad, besides 2521 in the naval, military, and Indian medical services, making in all 34,880. Of these only 268 are medical missionaries. While we may rejoice at the increase of the past sixty years, which shows a growth from 3 to 268, and especially of the last ten years, which shows an advance from 125 in 1890 to 268 in 1899, we can but ask if the sufferings of the heathen which have been briefly indicated in this chapter, and the splendid opportunities lying open to medical mission service, do not demand the consecration of many hundreds more to this invaluable agency for spreading the Kingdom of Christ upon the earth.[1]

---

[1] The figures are taken from *Medical Missions at Home and Abroad* for January, 1899; those previously given are from the same periodical for January, 1898.

Chapter VII.

Special Developments—Woman's Work in the Mission Field.

Woman's work in the mission field, as understood and organized to-day, is a very modern growth. It may be said to have sprung up almost entirely within the last sixty years, while the past twenty years have seen its most rapid advance and development. When Carey began his work in India the position of women in the heathen world was but feebly understood; while in western and enlightened lands the power and capacity of woman as teacher, evangelist, healer, and even leader, was undeveloped and scarcely imagined. It is only natural that the growth of woman's influence, combined with the great advance in her education which has been characteristic of the past thirty or forty years, should have manifested itself in the mission fields as conspicuously and beneficially as in other departments of human activity. The need of heathen women has been more fully recognized through the deepened contrast of the position of their western sisters; while the advance of the latter has provided in more ample measure the means of effectively bringing to the unenlightened the uplifting and saving influence of Christianity.

We must not forget, however, that long before the appointment of single women as missionaries, much splendid service had been rendered by the wives of missionaries, who not only shared their husbands' labours and perils, but were able as women to achieve much work that, under the conditions of heathen life, was entirely beyond the reach of men, however devoted and tactful. Through the presence of missionaries' wives, Protestant missions have been able to show the great object-lesson of a Christian home. The mutual trust of husband and wife, their helpful companionship, the brightness of their children's lives, and all the other elements that make the sweetness and charm of a Christian home have been, and are still, among the most potent influences for good in heathen lands. In India there are "houses, but no homes". "There exists", writes Sir M. Monier Williams, "no word that I know of in any Indian language exactly equivalent to that grand old Saxon monosyllable 'home'—that little word which is the key to our national greatness and prosperity. Certainly the word 'Zenana', meaning in Persian 'the place of the women', cannot pretend to stand for 'home' any more than the Persian 'Mandana', 'the place for men', can mean 'home'."[1] An equally significant commentary on Chinese customs and the position of Chinese women was the remark of some Chinese women who witnessed a marriage in a mission circle, "The bride looked pleased and happy". A Christian home has always been a wonderful phenomenon in heathen lands, and in any summary of woman's work the wives of missionaries must be recognized as some of the truest and most effective helpers, for it is no exaggeration to say that they do more than double the influence of a mission station. Amongst such labourers Mrs. Moffat may be mentioned, and the well-deserved tribute of her husband's words regarding her letters may be taken as typical of hundreds of others who have been true helpmeets:—"Into whatsoever letter I glance, there is the transcript of a soul sympathizing with and yearning to serve the interests of the Redeemer's Kingdom".[2]

[1] Quoted in *Our Indian Sisters*, by Rev. E. Storrow (London: Religious Tract Society), p. 64.

[2] *Heroines of the Mission Field*, p. 65 (containing also sketches of many others like-minded), by Mrs. Pitman. Cassell, Petter, Galpin, & Co.

The importance of the woman's movement abroad cannot be fully appreciated without a brief outline of the position of women in heathen lands. Among the many varieties to be found in the different nations and tribes, the condition of the many millions of women in India presents most strikingly the difficulty and urgency of this department of the missionary undertaking.

The first thing to be noticed is the contempt in which women are held, and the depravity with which they are credited under religious sanction. The answer of a Hindu who was asked if there were any points on which all—however sectarian—were agreed, "Yes, we all believe in the sanctity of the cow and the depravity of woman", is only too abundantly verified as regards the latter part by reference to Indian literature and the prevailing customs of Indian society. The following statement by Shoshi Chunder Dutt in his essays gives an appalling summary:[1]—"The position of women in India has hitherto been one of degradation and servitude. Though the legislators of Hindustan have not excluded females from Paradise, nor denied that they have souls, they have treated them in every respect with marked indignity and contempt, sparing no occasion to give vent to their scorn. While the minutest provisions are made in the Shastras for the mental cultivation of the boys, not even one stray text is to be found advocating the instruction of female children. On the contrary, women are in many places expressly refused access to the sacred scriptures of the country, and prohibited the acquirement of literary instruction, under a curse. The female who can read and write is branded as the heir of misfortunes. The Vedas are not even to be heard by women. And from the other sources of information they are also debarred, as, according to the authorities most commonly known and revered,

[1] Quoted from *Our Indian Sisters*, by Rev. E. Storrow, pp. 44-46.

the study of letters is considered a disqualification for domestic usefulness, and the sure inevitable harbinger of danger and distress. Women have accordingly received no education in this country, neither in childhood nor in youth, much less in maturer years.

"Nor is this all; not satisfied with debarring woman from mental cultivation, the lawgivers of India have also imputed unto her many of the worst propensities of human nature, and to her conduct attributed all the miseries of human life. 'Woman', say the Gentoo laws, 'is never satisfied with the gratification of her appetites, no more than fire is satisfied with burning fuel or the main ocean with receiving rivers.' Manu also tells us that women are always ready to corrupt men, whether wise or foolish. In the same strain says the Nit Shaster, 'To lie, to be impudent, to deceive, to speak bitter words, to be unclean and cruel, are all vices inherent in woman's nature, and most of all to find fault with a man if her wishes are not satisfied'.

"And the Vedas declare woman to be an incarnation of sin. . . . Nowhere has the national character been more low than in India, and nowhere has a worse opinion of female integrity been generally entertained."

Amongst the specific evils oppressing Indian women mention must first be made of those arising from the Zenana system. The Zenana is the portion of an Indian gentleman's house set apart for the women of his family. The rooms are generally bare and comfortless, and their inhabitants are without any cheerful or elevating occupation. Very few indeed of the Zenana women, who are believed to number 40,000,000, can read and write. Out of the 129,000,000 of women in British India, according to the 1891 census, only about half a million have acquired those arts, while some 200,000 more are learning them. "Their sole companions are near relatives, chiefly nieces, aunts, and sisters-in-law, some married, others unmarried, but all confined within the same restricted intellectual, social, and material horizon. . . . There is indeed an authority whose will is supreme —the grandmother, or mother-in-law, or sister-in-law, whose oriental conception of autocratic power is not likely to be softened by previous subordination, and still less by sweet reasonableness, the discipline of education, or the beneficent influence of a pure religion. . . . She is the enemy of all change and reform. Her government is a pure despotism, all the more harsh and overbearing because it is exercised for the most part over the daughters of other women."[1]

Mrs. Isabella Bishop has drawn from personal observation a saddening picture of Zenana life: "I have lived in Zenanas, and have seen the daily life of the secluded women, and I can speak from bitter experience of what their lives are—the intellect dwarfed so that a woman of twenty or thirty years of age is more like a child of eight intellectually; while all the worst passions of human nature are stimulated and developed in a fearful degree: jealousy, envy, murderous hate, intrigue running to such an extent that in some countries I have hardly ever been in a woman's house without being asked for drugs with which to disfigure the favourite wife or to take away the life of the favourite wife's son. This request has been made of me nearly one hundred times."[2]

Another evil in India is the prevailing custom of child-marriages, owing to which the great majority of girls are married before they are twelve years old, an immense number before they are ten, and many even at an earlier age. Closely connected with this, though by no means its only attendant sorrow and shame, are the practice

---

[1] *Our Indian Sisters*, p. 65.

[2] Speech in Exeter Hall, November 1, 1893. Published by the Church Missionary Society.

of polygamy and the treatment of widows, who are subjected to the cruellest indignities and not allowed by
custom to marry again.[1] The British Government has
done much to alleviate these woes, but no government,
however wise and humane, can meet the deepest needs of
all. The abolition of suttee under the direction of Sir
William Bentinck, in 1829, the educational policy of
1854 in favour of instructing women and girls, the
removal in 1856 of all legal barriers to the remarriage
of widows, and the laws against infanticide, deserve
honourable mention. Unhappily, only the first of these
has been entirely successful. Suttee is abolished, but
vast masses of women and girls are still illiterate, only
sixty remarriages of widows were recorded in all the
country up to 1886, and infanticide is far from being
eradicated. The elevation of women will only be accomplished by a revolution in public opinion in the
direction of Christian teaching and practice; and for
this is required not only the further and fuller enlightenment of men, but also continued and enlarged efforts
by women missionaries in many forms of Christian
service. The various societies have long recognized
that the work must be entrusted to specially-appointed
agents, for its vastness and complexity place it quite
beyond the reach of missionaries' wives, though they
have the honour of being its pioneers.

Turning to China, we find even more women than
in India, for they are estimated at 150,000,000. Their
condition may be summarized by saying that they
live in a heathen land, and so share the degradation
and oppression under which all heathen women —
the Japanese alone excepted—pass their lives. One
fact is sufficiently instructive. In China, a woman is a

[1] *Our Indian Sisters*, chapters vi., vii., and ix. See also *The High
Caste Hindu Woman*, by Pundita Ramabai Sarasvati. London: G. Bell
& Sons, 1888.

piece of goods to be bought and sold, and the horrors that surround that one fact are incapable of statement. At the same time Chinese women have remarkable power, and may be credited with having preserved the country, and with making themselves important factors both in political and social life.[1]   Hence the urgency of the call to enlighten and educate them, and the imperative need of women missionaries, who alone can reach them in their seclusion and ignorance and lead them to shake off heathen superstitions and customs.   Already, as stated elsewhere, there appears a native movement against foot-binding; but there can be no doubt that infanticide, especially in case of girls, is exceedingly common and in harmony with the public opinion of the country.

In Japan, woman has a far superior position to that which she possesses in India or China.   In many ways she approaches the influence and condition enjoyed in Western lands, but of course she needs—as the men of Japan—the sanctifying and renewing power of the gospel, and she can only fully receive it at the hands of Christian women.   It is a significant fact that forty per cent of the Christians in Japan are believed to be women.

In the uncivilized parts of the world woman shares the greater degradation of unrelieved darkness.   As the common drudge she is subjected to constant indignity and cruelty.   Here again she can only be liberated by her own sex, and though single lady missionaries are fewer than in India and China, they have most important and varied work before them which cannot be satisfactorily done by others.

The first advances towards ameliorating the lot of heathen women were made by the earliest missionaries

[1] Rev. W. S. Swanson, D.D., of the English Presbyterian Mission, Amoy. London Conference, 1888.   Vol. i. p. 400.

and their wives, among whom Mrs. Marshman of Serampore, and in later days Mrs. Wilson of Bombay, may be
mentioned in passing. More systematic efforts were
begun in 1819 by the establishment, at the instance of
some members of the Baptist Missionary Society, of the
Calcutta Female Juvenile Society for the education of
native females, and the formation of the Calcutta School
Society. Through the latter Miss Cooke went out in
1821; but before long she was transferred to the
corresponding committee of the Church Missionary
Society, under whose direction she rendered many
years' invaluable service. How little was accomplished
compared with the vast needs already indicated may
be imagined from the fact that in 1840 the number
of female pupils in Bengal was estimated at only 500.
It was reserved, however, for an American missionary
to give the impulse under which the first of the important women's agencies now existing in Britain was
formed. In 1834 the Rev. David Abeel, of the American
Board of Commissioners for Foreign Missions (Congregational), visited England on his way home from
China, and so powerfully described the condition of
women in India and China, and the need of employing
single women for their evangelization, that the Society
for Promoting Female Education in the East was instituted with the purpose of giving Christian instruction
to the women in the eastern hemisphere. This Society
may fairly claim to be the oldest Zenana Society, as in
1835 one of its ladies gained permission to teach in a
Zenana in Calcutta; but, owing to the great difficulties
in the way of such work, it directed its attention at first
chiefly to the aiding of female schools. The systematic
visitation of Zenanas came later, as we shall see. In
the last sixty years the operations of this society have
considerably expanded, and are to be found not only in
India and China, but also in Japan, the Straits, and the

Levant. It has also rendered service in Africa, Turkey, and Persia. Its present staff consists of 36 missionaries, including 1 medically qualified, and 107 native helpers.

The year of the Queen's accession witnessed the formation of the Scottish Ladies' Association for the advancement of Female Education in India. After the Disruption in 1843 this association became two: the Church of Scotland's Women's Association for Foreign Missions, which has now 36 missionaries, of whom 5 are medical, and 185 native helpers working in India, China, and Central Africa; and the Free Church of Scotland Ladies' Society for Female Education in India and South Africa, with 55 missionaries, including 5 medical, and 423 native workers.

While these important societies were beginning their honourable service, earnest appeals were not lacking for more systematic attempts to reach the secluded Zenana women, but they did not meet with much definite response till 1855. In that year the Bengal Missionary Conference heartily approved of the plans for Zenana visitation which had been adopted by the Rev. John Fordyce and Dr. Smith of the Free Church Mission, and declared that "it rejoiced in the hopeful commencement of the Zenana school system, both as a sign of progress and as a new means for the elevation of women in India". Prior to this, as has been said, Zenana work had been begun by the Society for Promoting Female Education in the East; and it should be added that such ladies as Mrs. Tracey in Benares, Miss Bird at Goruckpore and Calcutta, Mrs. Sale in Eastern Bengal, and Mrs. Mullens in Calcutta, had made similar efforts for Zenana women; but the credit of establishing the present Zenana mission system lies with the above-named earnest missionaries of the Free Church of Scotland.[1]

[1] See Storrow's *Our Indian Sisters*, pp. 212–214.

In 1851 some English ladies in Calcutta, through their interest in a young Hindu girl who had learnt the truth from reading the Bible and died a Christian at the age of seventeen, opened a training home for Eurasian teachers who might gain access to Zenanas and teach the Bible there. Having sent some money for the securing of a teacher to the Hon. Mrs. Kinnaird (afterwards Lady Kinnaird), and secured her warm sympathy and wide-reaching influence on behalf of the movement, they had the joy, in 1852, of establishing a Normal School in Calcutta and of being the means of forming in that year the Indian Female Normal School and Instruction Society. The constitution of the society, which was drawn up by the Rev. Henry Venn, at that time honorary secretary of the Church Missionary Society, provides for the union of Christians of all denominations for the four purposes of establishing Normal Training Schools, visiting Zenanas, conducting Vernacular Female Day and Boarding Schools, and training and superintending native Bible-women. In 1872 medical mission work was added, and subsequently village missions, which are carried on by bands of four or five missionaries living together in rural districts. In 1880 the Church of England Zenana Missionary Society branched off from this organization, and the original society assumed its present better-known title of the Zenana Bible and Medical Mission. It still retains its interdenominational character and works in co-operation with the Church Missionary Society, the Bible Society, and other Protestant agencies. Its present staff consists of 91 European agents, including 7 medical missionaries, and 267 native helpers. The superintendents of its work are connected with the Church Missionary Society, the Free Church of Scotland Mission, the London Missionary Society, and the American Presbyterians.

A Ladies' Auxiliary in connection with the Wesleyan Missionary Society was formed in 1859 for work among women in Ceylon (where it has met with its greatest success), India, China, and South Africa. It now maintains 50 European missionaries, including 1 medical, and 158 native helpers. Since this time similar organizations have been formed by the other leading missionary societies, though in some cases they are rather a development of the society itself than an association in connection with it.

The Universities Mission to Central Africa (established in 1859) first sent out lady missionaries in 1865, and now has 30 such workers in its fields. The same year also witnessed the beginning of the remarkable use made of women agents by the China Inland Mission, which is interdenominational. Not only is their number great, but their appointment as the only missionaries resident at many stations is almost peculiar to this mission. In some provinces they have been the pioneers. Between 1878 and 1881 women were able to enter and settle in six of the inland provinces, besides accomplishing journeys in Hunan, where permanent residence has only within the last two or three years been attainable. The number of ladies now on the staff is 258, of whom 1 is medical, with 77 native female helpers.

The Women's Missionary Association of the Society for the Propagation of the Gospel dates from 1867. Its present staff consists of about 80 missionaries, of whom 2 are medical, and 87 native helpers, in India, Burmah, Japan, Madagascar, and South Africa. Last year medical mission work was begun, and a dispensary was erected in Cawnpore.

The Baptist Zenana Mission, whose staff in India and China now numbers 64 missionaries, including 2 medicals, and 205 native workers, was formed in 1867.

The Irish Presbyterian Church, which took up this

work in 1873, has now a staff of 18 missionaries in India and China, 2 being medicals, and 126 native workers.

The London Missionary Society organized its female work in 1875, and now supports 69 missionaries, of whom 3 are medical,[1] in India, China, South Africa, Madagascar, and Polynesia, and 593 native helpers.

The Women's Missionary Association of the Presbyterian Church of England, started in 1878, has stations in China, India, and Morocco, and a staff of 22 missionaries.

The Church of England Zenana Missionary Society sprang in 1880 from the Indian Female Normal School and Instruction Society, from which it took over 31 missionaries working in seventeen stations. It now has the large force of 212 missionaries, of whom 7 are medical, and 743 native helpers. It works in close association with the Church Missionary Society in India, China, and Ceylon,[2] and as far as practicable at the same stations. The Church Missionary Society began sending out women missionaries in 1885, and though it has never adopted a formal resolution to send out such workers, it has now the splendid staff of 254 missionaries and 2004 native workers, who form the most striking addition of recent years to the ranks of women workers.

In connection with the United Presbyterian Church of Scotland, whose women's work was organized in 1880, there are now 42 lady missionaries, of whom 7 are medical, and 144 native helpers, in China, India, Old Calabar, and Kaffraria.

This brief summary of the societies which have the

---

[1] There are in addition four wives of missionaries, fully qualified, engaged in medical work.

[2] For admirable accounts of the C.E.Z.M.S. in India and China see *Behind the Pardah*, and *Behind the Great Wall*, by Irene H. Barnes. Marshall Brothers.

largest number of agents is sufficient to justify the statement that the growth in this agency has been one of the most remarkable in the past sixty years' history of our missions, for it shows that the number of women missionaries is now over 1500, while native women workers are rapidly nearing 6000. Thus a new form of organization has been added and developed for the raising of heathen women, which, at the beginning of this period, was only undertaken by missionaries' wives. In the meantime the wives of missionaries have become much more numerous, and in their enlarged numbers, amounting to over 1000, have continued their beneficent and devoted labours.

The scope and diversity of these labours may be briefly indicated in six divisions.

1. The visitation of Zenana and other secluded women has immensely developed since it was attempted in organized form. It is not possible to give either the number of houses visited or of the pupils who are instructed, but, as in all other departments of missionary labour, the need is far beyond the ability of the present staff, and the opportunities for such service are almost indefinitely increasing. At first Zenana missionaries had to gain admission by giving education or supplying school materials and books for nothing, by teaching needlework and other entirely secular pursuits; but now they are welcomed, or at least admitted, nearly everywhere as distinctly Christian teachers. In 1890 the number of houses open to Zenana teachers was 40,513. The instruction they give takes many forms, such as regular teaching on week-days and Sundays, Bible-readings, working parties, and gospel addresses. Ramabai, to whose sketch of *The High Caste Hindu Woman* reference has already been made, points out that the three great needs of her countrywomen are self-reliance, education, and trained native women teachers. Zenana

missionaries are ever working to supply these wants, and have many proofs that their labours are not wasted.

2. Closely connected with this branch is the training and superintending of native Bible-women and other helpers. As Ramabai says: "In a country where castes and the seclusion of women are regarded as essential tenets of the national creed, we can scarcely hope for a general spread of knowledge among women, either through men of their own race or through foreign women. All experience in the past history of mankind has shown that efforts for the elevation of a nation must come from within and work outward to be effectual. *The one thing needful, therefore, for the general diffusion of education among women in India is a body of persons from among themselves who shall make it their life-work to teach by precept and example their fellow-countrymen.*"[1]

No work is more important than the preparation of such native helpers, and all the Societies are earnestly endeavouring to supply the lack. A great many are already employed after more or less training. The Bible Society here again renders conspicuous service by supporting 504 native Bible-women in the East, of whom 428 work in connection with British societies. Through the labours of those at work in India it is estimated that 2000 women and girls are each year taught to read.

3. The production of literature suitable for women in heathen lands can only be effectively secured by the labours of those who are fully acquainted with their needs; and, as has been indicated in the chapter on literature, beginnings have been made both by female missionaries and native workers. At present, however, they are so overwhelmed with the mass of pressing calls for other kinds of work that the much-needed advance in literary service can hardly be expected.

4. The direct educational work undertaken in the

---

[1] *The High Caste Hindu Woman,* by Ramabai, p. 59.

several fields is not easily described owing to its great extent and variety. It comprises a vast number of elementary schools, orphanages for the bereaved and neglected, normal schools for training teachers, boarding-schools of various grades up to high-schools and colleges, homes for Christian women and for the training of Christian wives for native converts and teachers, Sunday-schools, and industrial institutions. While the maintenance and management of these various agencies have been shared by all the societies according to their ability and opportunity, the place of honour belongs to the Church of Scotland, which for sixty years in Calcutta, and for shorter periods elsewhere, has effectually promoted the education of women. In length of service the Free Church of Scotland has not been far behind, while its workers and schools have become more numerous than those of the body from which it sprang. The largest girls' school in India to-day, however, is the Sarah Tucker College of the Church Missionary Society, from whose operations the diversity and scope of such work in general may be best illustrated. "The Sarah Tucker College for native Christian girls at Palamcottah was founded in 1868 as a memorial of Miss Sarah Tucker, sister of the Rev. J. Tucker, Church Missionary Society missionary in Madras. It is worked by the Church of England Zenana Missionary Society, and in 1896 was raised from the rank of a training institution to the status of a second-grade college. There are 289 boarders and about 80 day-pupils in the present building; but the institution is in reality a net-work of agencies, since it has no fewer than thirty-six branch schools, two boarding-schools, two blind schools, two industrial classes, a little school for deaf and dumb children, and a small hospital." The main object of the college is to train the daughters of Southern India to become missionaries.

And to-day throughout Tinnevelly—a district the size of Yorkshire—Christian girls are to be found working earnestly and prayerfully as the mistresses of some fifty schools, attended by 2000 heathen children.[1] The results attained are at least sufficient to show the falsity of the Hindu saying that women have no minds.

The recent famine in India has made great additions to the numbers received in the orphanages of the different societies, and there can be no doubt that in the near future many who have thus been saved from starvation will go forth to break the bread of life among their countrywomen. Provision is constantly necessary for girls and women who, through breaking caste and embracing Christianity, are left destitute. Widows, too, often seek refuge from the hard conditions which native custom forces upon them, and find it in homes and industrial institutions. The teaching of industries to native women was introduced by Mrs. Mault (London Missionary Society) of Travancore, who before 1833 taught her pupils lace-making with great success. Since that time many other industries have been taught, amongst which embroidery and the spinning of cotton may be mentioned. Ramabai, whose remarkable history shows what a native woman can do, has established a home for child widows in Poonah, not in connection with any society, but with the deserved help of many friends in England and America. Her school was at first neutral towards Christianity, but has since become distinctly Christian.[2]

In this connection we may mention the work of the Indian Young Women's Christian Association, which endeavours to reach European girls away from home, domiciled Europeans and Eurasians, and educated native

[1] *Behind the Pardah*, pp. 153, 154.
[2] See *Across India at the Dawn of the Twentieth Century*, by Miss Guinness. London: Religious Tract Society, p. 89.

Christians.   In the past twenty years four central institutions have been opened in Bombay, Calcutta, Darjeel-
ing, and Madras.   These, with sixty-four branches, are
in the charge of 90 secretaries.   Some 200 meetings
are held each week, and 3000 members have been
enrolled.   The annual expenditure is £500.   It describes its parish as "100,000 English-speaking women,
and many hundreds of thousands of native Christians to
be reached in the vernacular".[1]   In other parts of the
world female education is not so highly developed as in
India, and has not yet been attempted on so large a
scale.   It has hardly passed beyond the elementary and
normal school, and the instruction of women and girls
in the ordinary decencies and duties of domestic life.
Beginnings have, however, been made in all the fields,
and are full of promise for the future.

5. Medical work among women is sorely needed, and
in the East must be done almost entirely by women.
The absence of real help in India from native doctors
led to the "National Association for Supplying Female
Medical Aid to the Women of India" (Lady Dufferin's
Fund), under the patronage of the Empress of India.
The medical missionary, as stated in chapter v., where
further reference to this department will be found, has
work of a higher kind to perform, and it is encouraging to know that at least fifty women holding British
diplomas are engaged in this service—in dispensaries,
hospitals, and home visits,—in addition to many more
who have been trained in elementary medicine, midwifery, and nursing, and are able to give much relief
and help amongst peoples so largely ignorant of these
subjects.   The training of native nurses and assistants
is going on apace, and there are cases of natives obtaining a full qualification in Britain and returning for
medical mission work among their countrywomen.

[1] See *Across India*, by Miss Guinness, pp. 136, 137.

6. Considerable attention has of late been given to evangelistic work in villages, especially in India and some parts of China. In the latter, the China Inland Mission has been conspicuous, as it regularly places ladies without men missionaries at many of its stations, the oversight of the converts and church organization being taken by ordained native pastors. Large and interesting work is also done in evangelistic tours in villages, and even towns, by the representatives of other societies. The vast majority of people in India are found in villages. The last census makes the urban population only 9·48 per cent, the rural 90·52. Two ladies will take up their residence in a village, and work in the adjoining district, assisted by native women. Sometimes they are found speaking to the great crowds that assemble at the fairs and festivals. In this branch of work, which is growingly useful, they have an advantage over men, because their audiences will contain both sexes, while male preachers usually gather only men to hear them.

Chapter VIII.

Special Developments—The Growth and Organization of Native Churches.

The ultimate object of the missionary societies described in this book may be stated in the admirable terms laid down in 1851 by the late Rev. Henry Venn, for thirty years the honorary and statesmanlike secretary of the Church Missionary Society, viz. "the development of native churches with a view to their ultimate settlement upon a self-supporting, self-governing, and self-extending system. When this settlement has been effected the mission will have attained its *euthanasia,* and the missionaries and all missionary agency can be transferred to the regions beyond." The purpose of this chapter is to indicate in outline the steps that have been taken towards this end, and to give some measure of the advance that has been made.

The task is not so easy as it might seem, owing to the very imperfect statistics obtainable for the year 1837, the variety of organization which has appeared in the mission field, and the difficulty of determining at what point in their development native churches may be precisely described as self-supporting, self-propagating, and self-governing. There is, however, a growing tendency to emphasize the duty of advance in these directions, and a satisfactory consensus of opinion among the workers of all societies that it is not their duty to reproduce in other lands exact copies of Western Church organization, or to attempt to stamp upon new churches the forms of Christian doctrine as they have been shaped by Western thought. Bishop Westcott has well said, "If we could establish the loftiest type of Western Christianity in India as the paramount religion—and it is, I believe, well-nigh impossible to do so—our triumph would be in the end a loss to Christendom. We should lose the very lessons which, in the providence of God, India has to teach us."[1] Yet it is obvious that to a large extent, for some time at any rate, native churches will naturally assume the forms of organization and modes of thought which characterize the leaders through whose agency they have been established.

The figures in the Appendix show the number of ordained native Christians in connection with the various British societies to be nearly 2000. That this is an immense increase since 1837 is clear from the fact that in that year there were only three such ministers con-

---

[1] *Religious Office of the Universities*, p. 33, quoted in the *History of the Church Missionary Society*, vol. ii. p. 426, by Mr. Eugene Stock.

nected with Church of England missions. The Society
for the Propagation of the Gospel had no clergy at that
time of other than European birth; in 1897 it had 178;
while the Church Missionary Society, to whom the three
already named belonged, had as many as 340. In con-
sidering the total figures of the Appendix, considerable
allowance must be made for churches in several parts
of the world which during the Queen's reign have
become practically independent of the societies by which
they were founded, and which may certainly claim to be
entirely self-supporting and self-propagating. It is very
difficult to say how far they may be regarded as self-
governing, owing to the influence unavoidably exerted
by European ministers, who form to a greater or less
extent part of the Council, Conference, or Union in
which they are organized. Amongst these the Wesleyan
Missionary Society,[1] which had missions in the South
Seas, West Indies, and British North America in 1837,
has been able to form Conferences which embrace all
the converts of these localities, and are entirely independent of the society. The number of members in
1837 was 61,914, which had grown to 457,203 in 1897.
Such figures give an illustration of the difficulty referred
to, for they contain the membership of the English-
speaking Wesleyans who are found in Australasia,
South Africa, and Canada, as well as that of the natives
of those countries. In the West Indies, again, the
figures given in the Appendix for the Baptist Missionary
Society take no account of the large number of natives
gathered into the 179 churches there, which, with a
membership of 34,140, form the Baptist Union of
Jamaica, which was started in 1848, and is entirely independent of the society. Similarly, the work of the
London Missionary Society in Jamaica has become

---

[1] Much work in the South Seas is carried on by the Australasian Wesleyan Missionary Society, formed in 1856.

independent of the society, and is now carried on by the Congregational Union of Jamaica, which embraces 24 churches. In Jamaica also the United Presbyterian Mission has greatly developed the native church, and its work is at present carried on by five presbyteries, comprising 60 congregations and 17 stations under the care of 2 European missionaries and 9 native ordained missionaries and 30 native evangelists. The membership is 11,247, and the contributions amount to £6823, which is some £3000 more than the expenditure met from home funds. It is interesting to note that these congregations provide the salary of one of the United Presbyterian missionaries in Rajputana, and give help also to the mission in Old Calabar. From British Guiana also the London Missionary Society has almost entirely withdrawn, having now only one missionary there. Its work is now carried on by the Congregational Union of British Guiana with 32 churches. In South Africa a similar state of things is found, where 30 churches, composed of natives gathered through the labours of the London Missionary Society, form part of the South African Congregational Union. Mention should also be made of the Presbyterian Church of South Africa, which aims at the complete incorporation of all the Presbyterian Churches there. At present, however, the Synod of Kaffraria, formed by the Free Church Mission, has not seen its way to enter the union. In the Kaffraria Synod there are 10 native churches, 103 branch stations, 6476 communicants, 12 ordained European missionaries, 2 native ordained pastors, 2 licensed native preachers, and 233 other native helpers. In all these cases, then, native churches have been established which are self-extending, self-supporting,[1] and self-governing, in accordance with the

[1] The small financial assistance given to some of the Congregational churches by the Colonial Missionary Society, and the presence of one

order and polity of the Christian bodies to which they belong. In view of these cases, then, the Wesleyan, Baptist, and London Missionary Societies may fairly claim in some of their fields to have attained the *euthanasia* described by Mr. Venn; they have been able to leave the work to the converts themselves, and to pass on to the regions beyond.

The nearest approach to this state of things in the Church of England Missions is perhaps found in connection with the Church Missionary Society's work among the Maoris in New Zealand. The beginning of that mission dates from 1814, and is associated with the honoured service of the Rev. Samuel Marsden. For eleven years no results were seen, but soon after 1830 the work grew rapidly, and the whole Maori nation was so effectively brought under Christian instruction that Bishop Selwyn, on his arrival in 1842, was led to write: "We see here a whole nation of pagans converted to the faith. . . . Where will you find throughout the Christian world more signal manifestations of the presence of the Spirit, or more living evidences of the Kingdom of Christ?" In 1859 the diocese of Waiapu was formed, and the Rev. William Williams, who had been for twenty years the chief missionary in that part of the country, was consecrated as bishop. Two years later he held a diocesan synod, which was entirely conducted in the Maori language. It was attended by 3 English and 3 Maori clergymen, and 17 Maori lay-delegates. The progress made is indicated by the formation in 1882 of a local Board of Bishops, Clergymen, and Laymen, which has since administered the grants of the Church Missionary Society, which are lessened each year, and will cease, subject to personal claims, in 1903. The work of the Church Missionary Society will

missionary (L.M.S.) in British Guiana, do not materially qualify this state-ment.

then be carried on by the New Zealand branch of the Church of England. The Maori clergy now number 39; there are 301 lay-teachers, 2450 communicants, and the native contributions for 1897 amounted to £1574.

In other colonies it will be found that the same state of things is repeated, the natives who are gathered by the different societies being in process of absorption in a Church the bulk of whose members are of British descent, so that, as Mr. Stock points out,[1] the *euthanasia* of a mission in a colony in which British settlers become the majority of the population is very different from the *euthanasia* of a mission in China or India or Equatorial Africa, where the white man is only a traveller or a sojourner. It is only in the latter that we can expect to see a really native Church which may in process of time develop on genuine native lines.

In the islands of the South Seas, where the London Missionary Society began its work a hundred years ago, there have long been entirely self-supporting churches. At the present time they have a membership of 14,899, and 268 ordained native pastors, while more than 350 men and women have gone as Christian teachers to New Guinea. Their contributions during 1897–1898 amounted to £4681. The society, however, has not yet seen its way to withdraw its missionaries and leave the native Churches to complete self-government and direction, nor is it likely that for some time to come it will be able to do so. For those who know the islands best maintain that never before was there such urgent need for keeping a guiding hand and maintaining a European supervision over the Christian life and work of these peoples. Grave difficulties have to be faced, which arise from their sensuous nature and their previous history, while new temptations assail them through sudden contact with modern civilization. The task of

---

[1] *History of the Church Missionary Society*, vol. ii. p. 84.

the missionaries still resident among them is to create a new Christian public opinion, to train their early perceptions of truth and duty into firmly-established principles of conduct, and especially to raise up a band of men with sufficient intelligence and moral strength to mark them out as the leaders of the native Church of the future.

Turning now to Western Africa, we have to record the remarkable progress made in connection with the work of the Church Missionary Society. In 1837 there were only 3 non-European clergy of the Church of England, and they were all found in Sierra Leone; now the number has grown to 16 in Sierra Leone, 26 in the Yoruba Mission, and 7 in the Niger Mission, making a total of 49, with 10,000 communicants; and in each of these districts the native Church has been organized with considerable success. The bishopric of Sierra Leone was established in 1852, and two years later the entire cost of the village schools, including the pay of 16 native teachers, and amounting to £800 a year, was thrown by the Church Missionary Society upon the native Church. In 1861, under a provisional constitution, nine parishes in the colony were formally declared to belong to the Church of Sierra Leone, each with its native pastor, supported by native Church funds, and responsible no longer to the society, but to the Bishop and Church Council only.[1] At the present time, under a constitution revised in 1890, the native Church has 12 native clergy, 94 native Christian lay-teachers, forty schools with 3711 scholars, 6473 native communicants, while the native contributions amount to nearly £4000 a year. In the Yoruba Mission the native Church presents the following figures: — clergy, 13; lay-teachers, 71; schools, 36; scholars, 2341; communicants, 238; contributions, £2614. Mention must also

[1] *History of the Church Missionary Society*, vol. ii. p. 101.

be made of the Niger Delta Pastorate Church, formed in 1891, which in 1897 had an income of nearly £1000, and which may claim to be "one of the agencies that are successfully solving the problem of the capacity of the negro for organization and self-government in ecclesiastical matters ".[1]

The most striking illustration of the capacity of the negro is afforded by the life and labours of Samuel Crowther, who, born in slavery, became the devoted Bishop of the Niger, and for more than twenty-five years (1864–1891) conducted with conspicuous ability and wisdom an African mission to African heathen.

In the populous land of India (excluding Burmah and Ceylon) the progress of missions during the forty years 1851–1890, so far as it can be given in statistics, is recorded in the following figures :—

	CHRISTIAN COMMUNITY.		COMMUNICANTS.				NATIVE AGENTS.	
	Number.	Rate of increase per cent.	Number.	Increase per cent.	Proportion of community.		Ordained.	Unordained.
1851	91,092	...	14,661	...	16·0		21	493
1861	138,731	52·3	24,976	70·3	18·0		97	1266
1871	224,258	61·6	52,816	111·4	23·5		225	1985
1881	417,372	86·1	113,325	114·5	27·1		461	2488
1890	559,661	34·0	182,722	61·2	32·6		797	3491

This table, which includes the figures of all societies at work in India, "shows not only that the growth of the Christian community has been very rapid, and that the Christian population is gradually overtaking the growth in the entire population of the country, but also that the work done has been thorough—intensive as well as extensive; for the proportion of communicants

[1] *The Lagos Echo*, January 15, 1898.

to baptized persons has been steadily increasing, which proves that the communicants—who may be regarded as well-instructed and consistent Christians—constitute an ever-increasing proportion of the native Christian community. . . . A further proof of the solidity of the progress of the native Christian community is seen in their steady advance in the social scale. The report of the Director of Public Instruction for the Madras Presidency contains the following passage:—'I have frequently drawn attention to the educational progress of the native Christian community. In the language branch of the B.A. examination, while the number of Brahmans examined in 1890 decreased by 8 per cent, the number of native Christians increased by 40 per cent. There can be no question, if this community pursues with steadiness the present policy of its teachers, that in the course of a generation it will have secured a preponderating position in all the great professions.'"[1]

While much encouragement may be derived from the foregoing figures—especially from the nearly fortyfold increase of the native ordained agents in forty years—we cannot form any opinion from them as to the position of the native churches in India with regard to self-government and self-support. We must judge of that from other considerations. It is satisfactory to find, amongst the missionaries in the field and the societies at home, a growing recognition of the importance of leading the native Christians in the direction of self-support and self-government. In 1858, at the Missionary Conference of Ootacamund, the matter was not discussed. At Bangalore, however, in 1879, and again in Bombay in 1892, it was a foremost topic; and it may be said that the old paternal system under which missionaries became pastors of native churches is com-

[1] Rev. E. P. Rice, B.A., in *A Primer of Modern Missions* (London: Religious Tract Society, 1896), pp. 58, 59.

pletely out of favour, and in every direction there is a determination not to do for the converts what they should obviously do for themselves, viz. provide and maintain their own places of worship, support the native ministry, and educate their children. But only very gradual progress can be expected, as "a church cannot easily be self-supporting while it forms a very small isolated community, especially when the majority of its members have come from the poorer classes, and those that had private means have been disinherited by the fact of adopting the Christian faith. And, as the Hindus have never been accustomed to self-government in any sphere, it is a work of time to teach them its responsibilities so as to make them independent of the European missionary."[1] The most advanced and systematic efforts in this matter have been made by the Church Missionary Society, and its native Church Councils deserve a brief description here. After the successful organization of the native Church in Sierra Leone in 1866, church committees for pastorates[2] were formed, with the pastor as chairman, and the members elected by the congregations. Their duties were defined as—"The general supervision and management of the temporalities of the congregations, the collection of funds, the superintendence of repairs of churches, schools, &c., the providing for the due performance of divine worship, and generally all such duties as belong to the office of churchwarden". District Church Councils were also formed, consisting of delegates from the various church committees, with the duties of receiving the church funds from the several church committees, and disbursing from the fund thus created the stipends of pastors and lay-agents, making

---

[1] Rev. E. P. Rice, B.A., in *A Primer of Modern Missions* (London: Religious Tract Society, 1896), p. 57.

[2] See *History of the Church Missionary Society*, vol. ii. pp. 420–421, whence this paragraph is taken.

grants for repairs, &c., supervising the work of unor-
dained agents, and recommending candidates for holy
orders. In some missions a Central Council was formed,
chiefly consisting of all the native pastors and of lay-
delegates from the District Councils, whose functions—
deliberative rather than executive—would be to consider
questions referred to them by the bishop or the Church
Missionary Society Mission, to make recommendations
to the District Councils regarding the administration of
their funds, and so help to unify the proceedings of the
Church. As the native Church could not meet all the
expenses, the society made a grant in aid, leaving the
native Church to make all the payments out of the
general fund thus secured. As the society's grant was
much larger than half the expenditure, the society appointed the chairman of the District Council, with a
power of veto upon its proceedings. The first chairmen
were naturally European missionaries, but in later years
native clergymen have in some cases been appointed.

In 1869, out of 50 native clergymen in South India,
42 were pastors working under this scheme; and beginnings had been made in Ceylon and Bengal. At the
present time the Tinnevelly District Church Council has
about 50 native clergymen, and takes charge of 817
native lay-workers, 12,433 communicants, 469 schools
with 3845 scholars, and an income of Rs.40,942. There
are six other similar Church Missionary Society Councils
in South India and Travancore, while the same organization has been established in Ceylon and Bengal.

Other societies also have moved in the same direction
on their own lines of organization in various parts of
the Empire. An attempt has also been made to establish
a national Church for India, but the twelfth annual
report (1897–98) shows that little advance has yet
been made: "There is nothing as yet visible prominently to note, yet we are glad to observe that our

efforts are enjoying the attention of thinking minds, and that the idea of the necessity there is for an indigenous Church is gradually spreading among the members of the Church of Christ".

The progress in China falls entirely within our period, for in 1837 there were practically no converts. The following figures, which are taken from the China Mission Hand-book for the year 1893, are for British societies alone: — ordained natives, 80; preachers, 527; other native workers (teachers, colporteurs, Bible-women, &c.), 1000; communicants, 27,206; organized churches, 371; self-supporting churches, 128; partly self-supporting churches, 261; and native contributions, $18,816. Since 1893 there has been a great increase in all the missions of the different societies; and were the corresponding figures available for 1897 they would show a considerable advance upon those given above.

The London Missionary Society, which was the first Protestant society to enter China, has found its most successful field in Amoy, where there are now 40 organized churches, of which 21 are wholly self-supporting, and 19 are partly so. Since 1892 especially, there has been a remarkable forward movement among these churches, through which the gospel has been carried into the large and unevangelized prefecture of Tingchiu. In the same part of China the English Presbyterian Mission has presbyteries at Amoy, Swatow, and in the Hakka country, to which we may add the presbyteries of Formosa and Singapore, giving a total of 14 fully-organized congregations, and 110 congregations not yet fully organized, with 13 native pastors supported by their own congregations in Amoy and Swatow. The Church Missionary Society's largest work is in the province of Fuh Kien, where pastorates have been formed and Church Councils established on the lines of their Indian and African Missions, and there are 10 ordained natives, 367 other native workers, and 3547 communicants. The Baptist Missionary Society had as many as 85 organized churches in 1893, and reports last year that "the desire to see an indigenous Church of Christ is being gradually realized. During the year the native pastorate and other expenses have been fully supplied from the triple source of labour, grain, and cash. It seems possible to establish an aggressive self-supporting cause, but it must be organized according to Chinese ideas. Without compromising in the least Scriptural principles, the Church here must be oriental in form of government, method of support and extension. But the question remains, how in the face of absolute poverty, a scattered membership, long distances, and bad roads, to organize and supervise spiritual teaching without compromising self-support." [1]

The Japan Mission is still more recent than the Chinese, dating from 1859, when American missionaries arrived there, and from 1869, when the first British missionary arrived in connection with the Church Missionary Society. In 1874 the United Presbyterian Church sent several missionaries to join in the promising work. In 1897 the adult Church membership was 40,578, who contributed 81,551 yen, while 3062 adults were baptized in that year. Under the new direction of the late lamented Bishop Bickersteth the "Nippon Seikokwai", or Japan Church, was formed, which unites in one ecclesiastical organization all the congregations connected with the Anglican Communion. The United Presbyterian Mission has joined with the American Presbyterian Church and the (Dutch) Reformed Church in forming the Union Church of Japan. The Church Missionary Society reports 1802 communicants, and the United Presbyterian Mission 892; the

---

[1] *Baptist Missionary Society's Report*, 1898, pp. 69, 70.

former has 14 ordained clergy, and the latter 2. The development of self-support, however, is very marked, as the above-mentioned contributions show; and the work of the Christian Church in Japan will soon be largely in the hands of the Japanese themselves.[1]

These particulars will suffice to show that the *euthanasia* of the missionary societies must not yet be expected. They have still in their most successful fields great work before them in guiding and directing the native Churches which have been formed; but they have ground for abundant encouragement as to the final success of their labours in the fact that the ordained natives now number nearly 2000, the other native helpers 48,000, while the Church members or communicants mount up to 340,000.

Chapter IX.

The Present Position.

The rapid and very imperfect survey of British foreign missions in the preceding pages has only touched the fringe of the subject, and has necessarily omitted many references to details. Yet the knowledge of details is essential to any true realization of the nature and extent of the work that is being done, or of the expenditure of brain and heart and all the finer qualities of life involved in doing it. One of the difficulties of the student of missions is that the work is now being done on so extensive a scale, and under such diverse conditions, that it becomes increasingly necessary to restrict the area of observation and to specialize study in one field, and even to the work of one society, if he would really become fully acquainted with the subject.

[1] *Primer of Modern Missions*, p. 154. R.T.S.

Elementary and imperfect as the review has been, it has sufficed to show how remarkable has been the expansion of the missionary enterprise during the past sixty years. The British Empire has grown to an extent unparalleled in history by the acquisition of territory and by colonial growth and expansion. The growth of the empire, however, has not been more remarkable than the growth of the Church in heathen lands. This growth is apparent in the extent of its operations, the variety of the means it employs, the results of its labours, and the increasing influence of the missionary idea in the Churches of Christendom. When the Queen ascended the throne far more than half the population of the world was inaccessible to Christian missionaries. Africa was unexplored. North America was out of reach. South America was impenetrable. The whole of Asia, with the exception of India, and to some extent Burmah and the Malay States, was closed. To-day, all these lands are open and accessible. Lines of steamers ply to ports whose very names were unknown sixty years ago, and trade is developing with peoples who were unthought of then. And wheresover the trader has gone, there the missionary has gone also, usually leading the way, and in not a few cases creating the conditions which were required for successful trade. British missions are world-wide in their extent, but withal they are wise in their economy of force. The missionary Church has learned in the presence of the overwhelming forces of heathenism to refrain from foolish rivalries and mutually injurious competitions between different sections of its workers. The principle of missionary comity has been recognized with increasing intelligence and loyalty by nearly all the societies and organizations at work in the mission field. They occupy by mutual arrangement, as far as possible, separate spheres of influence and areas of work, and are increasingly disposed to consult and act together for mutual benefit in those things in which united action or the adoption of a common rule is likely to be beneficial.

In 1837 missionary work was still in its elementary stage in almost every part of the field.   In the South Seas, the West Indies, and South and West Africa, which were as yet the most successful fields and those on which the greater part of the missionary force was concentrated, the Christian communities were still very young and immature, education was only beginning, literature was in its infancy, Church life was very limited, and local efforts in aggressive work had scarcely begun.   In each of those regions to-day the Christian community is strong in numbers, growing in intelligence, self-supporting, and to a large extent self-governing, and is actively engaged in missionary effort among others.   This, however, is only the smallest result of missionary enterprise during these sixty years.   A far greater and more important change has taken place.   There has been a complete shifting of the centre of interest and importance in the mission field. The earlier missions were undertaken, not because they were the most important, but because they were the most accessible.   The opening up of the world has brought the Church face to face with the vastly greater populations, the more difficult problems, and the more important interests of the great East.   The result is seen in the rapid development of the missions in India and China.   The population of those two countries numbers more than 600,000,000, *i.e.* more than half the non-Christian population of the world.   In their importance as a factor in the world's life they are far before the rest of the non-Christian races.   As these facts have been realized, increasing attention has been drawn towards them, and now fully two-thirds of the entire company of missionaries are employed in those two fields. The other and simpler fields have not been neglected, but the growth of Christian enthusiasm has produced an ever-increasing desire to work where the population is densest and where the intellectual and spiritual difficulties are most severe.

The growth in the number of workers has been re-markable. In 1837 there were about, but certainly not more than, 500. In 1897 the number had grown to upwards of 4000, of whom upwards of 1500 were Christian women. The results have been even more remarkable than the agency. Statistics give a very imperfect and unsatisfactory idea of these results, because the conditions of work in heathen lands are entirely different from those which prevail in Great Britain. The mind is consequently not furnished with the data for fair comparison where it is required to estimate results by statistics alone. It is true that as the result of the *pax Britannica* and all the advantages which accrue from good government, the heathen popu-lation of Her Majesty's dominions has increased by fully sixty or seventy millions during the Queen's reign, while the converts from heathenism in all parts of the world after a century of mission work probably do not number more than two millions. But to estimate the results of missionary efforts by such figures would be utterly misleading. What missions have effected for the elevation and improvement of the life of the world during the past sixty years can only be known when it is possible to estimate how much is involved in the diffusion of light, in the new influences introduced to family life, and in the physical and material improve-ments produced by the ministry of medical skill and the introduction of new industries. Three hundred and fifty thousand communicants in mission churches means that four hundred versions of the Scriptures in whole or in part have been prepared, fully two hundred of these

during the last sixty years by British missionaries, and
a new literature of Christian books has been begun, and
that the new, rich, and fruitful life of Christianity, with
its new sense of sin, its new ideas of truth and purity,
its new recognition of duty towards others, and its new
source of spiritual power, has been planted in the
wilderness of heathenism.   Five hundred thousand
scholars under Christian instruction represent the introduction of all these for the first time to the Book which
has done more than any other book or any other influence to cleanse and to ennoble the life of the country
which has sent out the missionaries, and which is daily
making the intellectual and moral contrast between the
enlightened and the unenlightened more marked.   Fifteen
hundred Christian women now engaged in bringing
Christian influence to bear upon the daughters, the
wives, and the mothers of heathen communities, are so
many agents of a great moral revolution, purifying thus
the fountains of the home life and creating new relations
to Christianity for the children of generations that are
yet to come.   Two hundred and fifty Christian medical
practitioners, labouring in love among the sick and the
diseased of the lands of ignorance, are not simply re-
lieving an enormous amount of suffering, and checking
the progress of disease, they are training a great company of skilled native physicians and midwives, and
through them are diffusing powers of healing in every
direction.   They are also dissipating the prejudice and
superstition which are the fruits of ignorance, and are
leading multitudes to associate all that is best in the
ministries of human help with a new conception of God
as compassionate love.   The missionary energy of the
past sixty years has sufficed by such means to set in
motion influences of enlightenment and of renewal which
will tell with cumulative force as the coming years
revolve.   It may be said without exaggeration that

sixty years ago the heathen world as a whole knew nothing of Christianity, and had not heard of Christ. To-day, as a result of the activities of this period of enterprise, Christian books have penetrated the most secluded and distant parts of the great East, the fame of the Christian teachers has spread to the centre of the darkest continent, and the influence of Christianity is showing itself for renewal and healing among the most degraded races.

The change of sentiment in relation to missions and the growth of missionary enthusiasm, and of the sense of responsibility for missionary service, in Britain and her colonies, have been as remarkable as the progress of missions abroad. This is seen in the number of organizations established for promoting mission work— of fifty-eight associations and societies named in the accompanying statistical table, only thirteen were in existence before Her Majesty the Queen ascended the throne. Yet the list given does not by any means represent all the agencies that are at work. Two movements of recent years are peculiarly significant and hopeful. The Young Men's Christian Association and the Young Women's Christian Association have during recent years extended their sphere of operations, and have discovered that one of the best means of promoting a healthy spiritual life among their members is to arouse their interest in the needs of the heathen. Not only are missionaries in various parts of the world supported by the members of these Associations, but similar organizations have been commenced through their energy, and that of the American associations, in various parts of the mission field. The Student Volunteer Missionary Union is the latest, and in many respects the most remarkable and promising, evidence of the wide-spread interest in missions and recognition of their claim on all Christians. The idea was started in the United States in 1886, but it speedily found hearty acceptance in Great Britain. Now there are upwards of 1634 students of both sexes, who are associated together by the very simple yet significant pledge, "It is my purpose, if God permit, to become a foreign missionary". These students are to be found at all the great national universities, as well as in theological colleges, normal colleges, and schools of medicine. They number among them many who are giving marked evidence of ability. They are promoting the study of the literature of missions by meeting in missionary bands and classes, and by the preparation of excellent manuals. They maintain and stimulate interest in missions by meetings and conferences, and more than one special effort to establish university settlements in India has sprung from the ranks of the volunteers.

Another evidence of the place which foreign missions have gained in the thought and interest of the Church is to be found in the remarkable growth of missionary literature. Not only is this to be seen in the number and variety of monthly magazines and occasional papers of various kinds issued by the missionary societies for the information and interest of the public, but also in the rapid multiplication of books on missionary subjects. The bibliography of missions published in the Report of the Conference on Missions held in London in 1888, extends to forty-eight pages, octavo. It is true that these are not all books from a missionary standpoint or on missions. There are not a few books of travel or histories of the countries in which missionaries are working, and a considerable proportion of the whole are American or Continental. Fully half, however, are by British authors, many of them missionaries, and are on subjects relating to missions. Every year adds largely to such literature, historical, biographical, or dealing with the great subject of missions from some special point of view.

Prayer unions, numbering many thousands of members, who are pledged to regular intercession for missions, have been formed in connection with the Church Missionary Society, the China Inland Mission, the London Missionary Society, the Wesleyan Missionary Society, and several other organizations. The formation of these associations has led to a great increase in the study of missionary literature, and has largely aided in sustaining and diffusing an interest in missions.

Contributions to the support of missions have increased fivefold during the period under review. They are now received from a much larger area and much more systematically. Local associations and societies have been formed in Canada and in various parts of Australia which are providing workers and funds in steadily increasing quantity.

Much might be said of the effect this increase of Christian activity, and this growing knowledge of the moral and spiritual conditions prevailing in the great heathen world which Christianity has to meet and change, has had upon the thought and life of the Church at home. Unquestionably the vision of the vast extent of the heathen world, and the experience of the difficulty of work in it, have insensibly affected the opinions of the most rigid interpreters of the Divine decrees. The views of Christians as to the Divine purposes of salvation have broadened, and the meanings they attach to the great doctrines of grace have been modified and enlarged. Unquestionably also a richer spiritual experience and a stronger faith have come to those who have recognized the responsibility and privilege of this larger service. The Churches which have been most enthusiastically missionary have been most fruitful in work for those at home.

It cannot be said that the effort to fulfil "the great commission" has yet become the central thought and purpose of all Christians, but a great and marked change has taken place. Sixty years ago the majority were uninterested if not still unbelieving, to-day the majority accept the duty of carrying the Gospel to the heathen as a recognized part of their creed, and a considerable number are endeavouring to embody their creed in consecrated service. The hope of the future is that the young life of the Churches is manifesting an increasingly intelligent and earnest interest in the progress of missions.

Index.

Index. 229